HOW TO
MAKE A
SERIAL
KILLER

HOW TO MAKE A SERIAL KILLER

THE TWISTED DEVELOPMENT OF INNOCENT CHILDREN INTO THE WORLD'S MOST SADISTIC MURDERERS

CHRISTOPHER BERRY-DEE
AND
STEVEN MORRIS

Ulysses Press

Published in the United States by
Ulysses Press
P.O. Box 3440
Berkeley, CA 94703
www.ulyssespress.com

First published in the U.K. in 2006
as *Born to Kill?* by John Blake Publishing

ISBN13: 978-1-56975-654-6

Library of Congress Control Number: 2007907745

Printed in the United States by Quad/Graphics

3 5 7 9 10 8 6 4

Acquisitions: Nick Denton-Brown
Editorial: Amy Hough, Emily Reed, Abigail Reser, Emma Silvers
Production: Lisa Kester, Judith Metzener
Cover design: Double R Design
Cover photo: Lorraine Swanson

Dedicated to Patrick Dee 1917-2005

ACKNOWLEDGMENTS

How to Make a Serial Killer came about after Christopher Berry-Dee was invited to appear on the British 2005 Sky TV series *Born To Kill?* The TV series raised and discussed many issues and it seemed only logical to expand them further to create a book. A TV series can often be a here-today-and-gone-tomorrow phenomenon, whereas books last. The aim of this book is to be something that anyone interested in the subject can return to again and again in an effort to understand the mind of the serial killer.

As with any book, the authors are delighted to give due credit and acknowledge those who have contributed to the project, and we start by thanking those who have supplied valuable information, and who have appeared throughout the TV series.

Ivan Milat: Paul Kidd, author *Australian Serial Killers*; Mark Whittaker, co-author *Sins of the Brother*; Mark Tedeschi, Crown Prosecutor; Peter Cantarella; George Milat; Don Borthwick; Jacquie and Ian Clarke; Commander Clive Small; Dr. Rod Milton; Neil Mercer, *The Sunday Telegraph*; Terry Martin, Milat's defense lawyer.

Fred West: Dr. David Holmes; Jean Ritchie; Brian Masters, author of *She Must Have Known*; Dave Newman; Anthony Daniels, author of *So Little to be Done—The Testament of a Serial Killer*; Leo Goatley, Fred West's solicitor; Hugh Worsnip; Caroline Owens; Professor Bernard Knight, pathologist.

Jeffrey Dahmer: Patrick Kennedy, Milwaukee PD; Colonel Robert Ressler, FBI; Michael McCann, District Attorney; Gerald Boyle, Dahmer's attorney; Tony Timer; Nico Claux, convicted murderer and cannibal; Sopaxliba Princewill, Dahmer's landlord; Dr. David Holmes; Roy Ratcliffe.

Myra Hindley: Dr. David Holmes; Jean Ritchie, author of *Mind of a Murderess*; Geoff Knupfer, former Chief Superintendent Greater Manchester Police; Marie Cheffings; Elizabeth Cummings, former acquaintance of Myra Hindley; Laurence Jordon; Danny Kilbride, brother of victim John Kilbride; Winnie Johnson, victim Keith Bennett's mother; Tony Brooks of the *Manchester Express*; Andrew McCooey, solicitor for Hindley, *circa* 1982; Linda Malvern.

ACKNOWLEDGMENTS

The Washington Snipers: Sergeant Roger Thomson, Montgomery County Police; Jon Ward, *The Washington Times*; Dr. Dewy Cornell, attorney for John Mills; Sonia Wells; Chrissy Greenawalt; Detective Ralph Daigneau, Prince William County Police; Dr. Evan Nelson; Vickie Snider; Roger Holmes, long-time friend of John Muhammad.

Dr. Harold Shipman: Dr. David Holmes; Bernard Postles, Detective Superintendent Greater Manchester Police; Mikaela Sitford, author of *Addicted to Murder*; John Pollard, Chief Coroner; Brian Whittle, author of *Prescription for Murder*; Ann Alexander, solicitor for families in the Shipman enquiry; Bob Studholme; Mike Heath; Dr. Michael Grieve; Colin Shotbolt; Tony Fleming.

Much appreciation goes to TV series producer Charlotte Wheeler (Charlottski), and researchers Jon McKnight and George Hughes. Also to Jane Geran and Jason Langley, along with all those at TwoFour Productions who made the TV series possible. And, of course, John Blake and Lucian Randall at John Blake Publishing.

The authors' personal thanks go out to Kirstie McCallum and Nancy Holloway for supporting us, also specifically to warm-hearted Elaine Anstess, Tatiana, Sasha, Zoe, Joanna Dee and all of the team at *The New Criminologist*, www.newcriminologist.co.uk. Thanks also to Nick Morris, Marilyn and Scott Dorrall.

CONTENTS

INTRODUCTION

"It looked like I would never be punished by God or Satan, and when we died our lives just flickered out. The sooner a person understands that there's no punishment after death and allows their own impulses to take over, the sooner they become an unstoppable serial killer. That's the point I'd reached. It was scary, but it was exciting too."

Keith Hunter Jesperson, "Happy Face Killer,"
from *The Creation of a Serial Killer* by Jack Olsen

THIS BOOK ASKS—and tries to answer—the fascinating question: Are we born to kill? Within that, many more equally compelling questions are raised: If we are born to kill, does this mean that some of us are destined to be killers and that there is nothing society can do about it? Or can something be done? On the other hand, if it is a case of nurture rather than nature, how are serial killers "made?" Do they all follow the same path of development or do different circumstances create different types of serial killers?

When TwoFour Productions put together the idea for the six-part TV documentary series *Born to Kill?* the original concept was for myself and my co-author Steve Morris to write a book to accompany the series. However, it quickly became clear that any book we wrote could go beyond the scope of the series and really pose some interesting questions about the nature of serial killers. Together with Jason Langley, the Commercial Director at TwoFour Productions, and our publisher John Blake, Steve and I began to discuss putting together what we now believe to be one of the most important books of its kind available today.

The authors' brief was to follow the format of the TV series, thus we have included the principal characters to form the backbone of the text: Frederick and Rose West, Dr. Harold Shipman, John Muhammad and Lee Malvo, Jeffrey Dahmer, Ian Brady and Myra Hindley, and Ivan Milat. However, myself and Steve—with his immense knowledge on the subject of sexual serial homicide—soon realized that also including the histories of several other serial murderers in this book would add far greater socio-criminological value, especially when weighed alongside the more recent scientific studies concerning the nature vs. nurture debate.

Wherever you stand on this debate, the one thing to bear in mind is that it is an issue that concerns every one of us, especially anyone with children. We would even go so far as to say that every parent should read *How to*

Make a Serial Killer because it is a wake-up call and its findings could change the way we look at what makes a killer. It is, we conclude, not a case of nature vs. nurture but nature *and* nurture.

Unusually for a true-crime book, we have set out to devote more space to the offenders' early histories and less space to their actual crimes. After all, we reasoned, the question really being asked here is: How do these monsters develop into killing machines in the first place? Are they born to kill, bred to kill, taught to kill or trained to kill? Is there really a "demon seed" within some of us that ensures we are preprogrammed to commit serial homicide from conception?

Despite the undoubted wickedness of the killers featured throughout this book, we have shown them some compassion where we feel it is appropriate. In my travels around the world, especially in the U.S., I have always been mindful of how law enforcement officers, attorneys, the judiciary and even the next-of-kin of the victims often refer to these murderers by their Christian names. My first experience of this came about when I was researching Henry Lee Lucas. I interviewed Sheriff Bill F. "Hound Dog" Conway in his office at the Montague County Jail. With his leather-tooled cowboy boots planted up on his desktop, and surrounded by a veritable arsenal of weaponry from six-shooters to assault rifles, "Hound Dog," in his north Texan drawl, always referred quite affectionately to Lucas as "Ole Henry."

No matter who the killer was, no matter what atrocities these people had committed, from state to state, jurisdiction to jurisdiction, it was always the same: Aileen Wuornos became "Lee," and Kenneth Bianchi was simply "Ken." While I was consulting with the Metropolitan Police on the killer John Cannan, DCI Jim Dickie and DI Stuart Ault always called Cannan either "Mr. Cannan" or "John." At a temperature of -18 degrees, while interviewing through a misty camera lens inside Russia's toughest female prison at Sablino, the governor referred to her charges as Victoria, Katya or Svetlana. These women were ruthless serial killers. One of them was even a cannibal—and had bizarrely been appointed head cook in the prison's kitchens.

You will find in this book that the killers are often referred to by their first names, too. There is a good reason for this. Mindful as we are of the disgusting crimes they have committed, aligned with the heartbreak and distress they have caused to thousands of people, we should also assert that serial killers are, like all of us, human beings, too. They were born into the world, for the most part, as innocent children. But unlike the majority of us, almost from the cradle their lives and personalities were abused and distorted by their parents and caregivers. We cannot blame serial killers for this aspect of their lives, at least. This is the approach we have adopted throughout the book. We apportion blame where necessary but we also show compassion or understanding where we believe it is right to do so.

Throughout the book we hope to show how widely different backgrounds and upbringings can lead to the same result—an unrepentant serial killer. The final, lengthy chapter concerns itself with one of America's most notorious sado-sexual serial killers, John Wayne Gacy. You will see how his boyhood was completely the opposite of someone like Fred West, but how they both became monsters. At the same time, you will also see how others were almost like two peas in a pod. The lesson will be that there is no one route to becoming a serial killer and no easy assumptions to be made. We want our readers to enjoy this often-shocking book, while learning valuable lessons at the same time.

In *How to Make a Serial Killer* we suggest that by examining the past histories of the offenders included in this study we may learn more about the potential outcomes of a negative and abusive upbringing. We hope that this will help to prevent the emergence of serial killers, spree killers and mass murderers in the future.

Christopher Berry-Dee
Group publisher *The New Criminologist*
www.newcriminologist.co.uk
May 2006

CHAPTER 1

NATURE VS. NURTURE

BORN TO KILL, bred to kill, taught to kill or trained to kill? These are questions that need to be asked and answered if we are to understand a serial killer's career.

Although it may sound like a strange word to choose, "career" is correct. It's as much of a career as any other. Some people choose it, while others say it was something they were born to do—just as much as with any other career, only here the context is so strange that it is difficult to think of serial killing as a life choice. But stop and think for a moment and substitute the words "serial killer" for any other type of career. Do we question whether other people were "born" to their careers or chose them in later life?

Do we ask whether a bus driver was predetermined to do his job? The consequences of growing up to become a bus driver are simply not interesting enough to a wide sector of society to give the question much thought. The same applies to more high-profile jobs. Few questioned if the late Pope John Paul II was "born" to his papal calling, or how Dr. Christiaan Barnard arrived at his career choice as a pioneering heart transplant surgeon. It is arguable that the minds of such high-flying "good" people are as worthy of study as those of serial killers. However, the one thing the story of a "good" person lacks over that of a "bad" person is the grim fascination we associate with the deeds of the latter. We do not need to know why a "good" person is good. We are simply happy that they are. But we do, at some basic level, need to know why "bad" people are bad. By understanding the dark side of human nature we feel we can protect ourselves from it in some way.

This is what we aim to do in this book. Take the British serial killer Fred West, for example, who on the surface was a freelance construction worker from Gloucester. He was undoubtedly one of the most sick, twisted and perverted serial murderers that ever lived. Speaking in terms of a pack of cards, the authors award him the "Ace of Spades." We claim that not only was he born to kill, he was also bred and taught to kill as well. He was a very particular type of serial killer, as evil as they come.

Next, look at Myra Hindley, one of the most reviled women in British history. We argue, in what may be an unpalatable truth to some, that had she not met her partner-in-crime, Ian Brady, it is doubtful she would ever had killed anyone. The fact that they both worked at the same engineering firm was the unhappy accident that set off a tragic train of events. Hindley, we believe, learned to kill. She was not, as the phrase has it, a "natural born killer."

Then there is the case of Dr. Harold Shipman. A general practitioner in the Manchester, England area, "Dr. Death" was trained to save lives and ended up turning his medical education on its head. He is suspected of approximately two hundred and fifty murders, making him perhaps the world's most prolific serial killer. Many authorities suggest that he may in fact be responsible for up to one thousand deaths. Whatever the actual figure, he eclipses the toll of any other serial killer caught to date and he is as different a type of serial killer from Fred West as he is from Myra Hindley.

John Allen Muhammad and Lee Malvo, a.k.a. "The Washington Snipers," offer another contrast similar in some ways to Brady and Hindley yet different in many others. John had been trained to kill as a U.S. soldier and, in turn, took it upon himself to train seventeen-year-old Lee Malvo as a sniper. Together they shot over twenty-five people, killing at least fifteen.

Jeffrey Dahmer, "The Milwaukee Cannibal," was outwardly an ordinary worker at the Ambrosia Chocolate Factory in Milwaukee. Yet he enticed his victims to his home, where they were drugged, strangled and then dissected. His actions suggest that his motives were more to do with a fascination for mutilation than loneliness or any of the other reasons usually assigned to the acts of a serial killer.

Finally, there is Ivan Milat, the "Australian Backpack Killer," an itinerate drifter who lived off his wits, robbing banks to pay his way. With seven confirmed kills, and possibly as many as twenty-eight, Milat was the stereotypical sado-sexual serial killer. One of a breed that does not simply emerge overnight, Milat's development followed a career path that led from petty crime, through to sexual assault, rape, serial rape and then to murder.

But can we suggest that any of the names from this hall of infamy were born to kill? Maybe yes, maybe no. With the exception of Myra Hindley and the Washington Snipers we can say, with more than a degree of certainty, that there was within each of them a latent predisposition to commit multiple murders.

It is a long-established fact that the structure and quality of family interaction is an important part of a child's development, especially in the way the child itself perceives family members. According to the FBI, "For children growing up, the quality of their attachments to parents and to other members of the family is most important as to how these children, as adults, relate to and value other members of society. Essentially, these early life attachments (sometimes called bonding) translate into a map of how a child will perceive situations outside the family."

For some time we have known that human development results from the dynamic interplay of nature and nurture. From birth, we grow and learn because our biology is programed to do so and because our social and physical environment provides stimulation.

During the first three or four years of life—the formative years—children experience the world in a more complete way than children of any other age. Their brains take in the external world through its system of sight, hearing, smell, touch and taste. This means that infant social,

4

emotional, cognitive, physical and language development are stimulated during multisensory experiences. Infants and toddlers need the opportunity to participate in a world filled with stimulating sights, sounds and people.

Unfortunately, early development does not always proceed in a way that encourages a child's curiosity, creativity and self-confidence. For some children, early experiences are neither supportive nor predictable. The synapses that develop in the brain may be created in response to chronic stress, or other types of abuse and neglect. When children are vulnerable to these risks, problematic early experiences can lead to poor outcomes. For example, some children are born with the tendency to be irritable, impulsive and insensitive to emotions in others. When these children's characteristics combine with adult caregiving that is withdrawn and neglectful, their brains can wire in ways that may result in unsympathetic child behavior. When these children's characteristics combine with adult caregiving that is angry and abusive, their brains can wire in ways that result in violent and overly aggressive child behavior. If the home environment teaches children to expect danger instead of security, then poor outcomes may occur, as this book will show. In these cases, how do nature and nurture contribute to early brain development?

More recent research tells us that early exposure to violence and other forms of unpredictable stress, as experienced by many of the killers featured in this book, can cause the brain to operate on a fast track. Such overactivity of the connections between the brain's axons and dendrites, combined with a child's vulnerability, can increase the risk of later problems with self-control. Some adults who are violent and overly aggressive experienced erratic and unresponsive care in early life.

Adult depression can also interfere with infant brain activity. When parents suffer from untreated depression they may fail to respond sensitively to infant cries or smiles. Adult emotional unavailability is linked with poor infant emotional expression. Infants with depressed caregivers do not receive the type of cognitive and emotional stimulation that encourages positive early brain development, because they learn to "mirror" the mood swings and negative anxieties expressed by the parents.

IN OUR GENES?

In today's more enlightened times, social scientists increasingly appreciate the extent of the interactions that take place between nature and nurture. They have discovered that the presence of genes does not, by itself, ensure that a particular trait will be manifested because genes require the proper environments for innate tendencies to be fully expressed. These "proper environments" consist not only of natural surroundings but also of individuals' social and symbolic milieus.

Simply put, there may well be a faulty gene inbred amongst millions of us; but for the better part of the time it remains latent, fenced-in by a happy childhood based on a solid family upbringing.

Recently, it has been revealed by British scientists in a study of 3,687 pairs of seven-year-old twins that there are strong genetic roots for poor behavior in children who also showed signs of psychopathic traits, such as lack of remorse or understanding for the feelings of others. This research, carried out at King's College London, also points to environmental factors, such as social and family background, as the chief cause of antisocial activity among a larger group of badly behaved children. Dr. Essi Viding of the college's Institute of Psychiatry, who led the study, said it suggested that much teenage antisocial behavior has its origins earlier in life and that efforts to prevent it need to begin at a young age. Writing in *The Times* in May 2005, Science Correspondent Mark Henderson put things more succinctly when he wrote: "Some yobs are born; others are made."

Even when children have a genetic predisposition to such problems, they are likely to respond to environmental triggers that could be reduced by early intervention. Research led by Temi Moffitt, one of the King's College team members, has established that boys with a particular version of a gene called MAOA are more likely to grow into antisocial adults, but only if they are also maltreated as children.

In his findings published in *The Journal of Child Psychology and Psychiatry* in May 2005, Dr. Viding investigated children classed by their teachers as among the most antisocial and disruptive 10 percent, and split them into two groups. One of the groups showed psychopathic or "callous-unemotional" traits, such as a lack of empathy and guilt, while the other group did not.

In the callous-unemotional group, antisocial behavior was about 81 percent heritable—meaning that four-fifths of the differences between them and the general population appear to be explained by genetic factors. Genetic influence on antisocial behavior in the other, larger group was much lower—heritability was about 30 percent, with the remaining variability explained by environmental factors.

The research carried out in London has also been supported by the findings of an international team of researchers that followed a group of 1,037 children born in 1972 in Dunedin, New Zealand. Their study focused on the MAOA gene that produces an enzyme that is important in breaking down neurotransmitters linked with mood, aggression and pleasure. This particular gene comes in a strong and a weak variant. The study found that 85 percent of the male children who had the weak variant of the MAOA gene and who were abused while growing up exhibited criminal or antisocial behavior. This was a rate nine times greater than was found among similarly-situated males with the strong version of the gene.

An excellent example of a serial killer who had this weak variant of MAOA influence is Michael Ross. Executed in Connecticut on May 13, 2005, Michael became a sado-sexual psychopath who raped and murdered eight women, including two schoolgirls. I affirm that Michael was most certainly wrongly "wired-up" in the hypothalamic region of the limbic system, the most primitive and important part of the brain. The hypothalamus serves the body tissues by attempting to maintain its metabolic equilibrium and providing a mechanism for the immediate discharge of tensions. It appears to act like an on/off sensor, on the one hand seeking or maintaining the experience of pleasure and, on the other, escaping or avoiding the experience of pain or unpleasantness.

If, for example, the hypothalamus experiences pleasure, be it from satisfying a craving for chocolate, drugs or sex—even the need for sadistic sexual murder—it will switch on "reward" feelings so that the person continues engaging in the activity. If it begins to feel displeasure, it will turn off the reward switch. But, if the switch jams halfway, so to speak, the limbic urge goes unmet, and the individual will experience depression, anger or even homicidal rage.

This was most certainly the case with Mr. Ross, who I suggest was born to kill, bred to kill and who subsequently, learned to kill.

XYY CHROMOSOME DISORDER?

The New York serial killer Arthur Shawcross, dubbed by the media "The Monster of the Rivers," suffers from what he calls "a rare genetic disorder." I interviewed him twice at the Sullivan Correctional Facility, in September 1994.

This claim made by Shawcross—which is substantiated by many of America's leading authorities in the field who subscribe to the theory that XYY abnormalities may be the cause of violent and homicidal behavior—confirms that he is certainly suffering from an extremely rare biochemical imbalance linked to a rare XYY genetic disorder. It is contended that this genetic mix could be at least part of the reason why he commited such antisocial acts of violence.

Looking back to his formative years, there was well-documented evidence even then to show that Shawcross was displaying signs of antisocial behavior during this period of his life. We know he was bullied before the tables finally turned and he became a bully and sadist himself. The roots of his evil had already been planted by this time. Indeed, this genetic disorder was within him from conception and might account for him being the only rotten apple in a basket of otherwise good fruit in regard to the rest of his family.

When I questioned the prison medical officer on this issue the doctor declined to confirm that Shawcross had any such problem. But Dr. Kraus, who spent months evaluating Shawcross, found solid evidence that Arthur does indeed have an XYY disorder. When I approached several of the world's leading authorities seeking clarification on the XYY phenomenon linked to antisocial behavior, not surprisingly I received no clear answer.

With our present state of knowledge, it seems that chromosomal abnormality can only have a bearing on a minute fraction of the criminal population, and it is also necessary to consider the millions of people throughout the world who have an XYY abnormality and who exhibit no antisocial tendencies whatsoever. Consequently, while an XYY disorder might partly account for Shawcross's behavior it cannot provide the total picture.

There are a hundred million brain cells in the average person, and the presence of one extra chromosome in each cell equates to the presence of an additional one hundred billion chromosomes in the XYY male not normally present in the normal XY male.

World-respected geneticist Dr. Arthur Robinson once screened 40,000 newborns for XYY, and he has claimed that about 2,000 XYY males are born in the U.S. each year. His research shows that two-thirds are thin, tall and awkward, with an IQ range of 80–140. Dr. Robinson says, "These people are excitable, easily distracted, hyperactive, and intolerant of frustration. Fifty percent are learning disabled (compared to 2–8 percent in the general population) and most suffer delays in speech development." Many of these personality characteristics uncannily match Shawcross's profile.

Dr. Kraus has commented, "Studies report that the XYY male has a ten- to twenty-fold increase in his lifetime risk as compared to their incidence in the population of being institutionalized in a mental hospital or prison—a risk that is not trivial. XYY males have a much higher average rate of learning disability and are described as "problem children" who cause serious behavioral and management problems at home and school. Studies describe how at least some XYY boys show behavioral disability that makes them not only a great problem in family management, but also quite disparate from other family members in their behavior altogether." This is a finding consistent with the early life history of Arthur Shawcross and his own frequently-reported belief that he was "different" from the rest of his family members.

Personality characteristics associated with these children also describe them as drifters or loners disposed to running away from home, who, as they grow up, are frequently agitated, experiencing pedophilic urges, setting fires, threatening to kill others, molesting children, stealing and exhibiting moments of sudden violence and

aggression. These are all the personality traits well documented in Shawcross's life.

In an article entitled "Human Behavior Cytogenetics,"
published in the *Journal of Sex Research*, Dr. John
Money adds weight to Dr. Kraus's claim. Dr. Money wrote,
"It seems perfectly obvious that an extra chromosome in
the nucleus of every cell of the brain somehow or other
makes the individual more vulnerable to the risk of developing mental behavioral disability or abnormalities."

It seems that at the very least an XYY chromosome
disorder is part of Shawcross's problems. But what of the
biochemical imbalance? In searching for a diagnosis in
Shawcross's case Dr. Kraus turned his attention to blood
and urine testing, where he hit upon a little-known fact
revolving around kryptopyrrole. Indeed, so little was
known about kryptopyrrole that half of the authorities
Dr. Kraus spoke to for advice had never heard of it, and
the biochemistry laboratory at the University of
Rochester didn't know how to spell the word, replying,
"It sounds like something out of a Superman movie,
doesn't it?"

During laboratory examination of Shawcross's bodily
fluids, Dr. Kraus found that while the concentrations of
copper, zinc, iron and histamines were all within the normal range expected to be found in a healthy person, one
of the results from an analysis of urine showed unexpect-
ed findings. Kryptopyrrole showed H 200.66 mcg/100cc
against an expected value 0–20. The "H" was laboratory
shorthand for "High."

Kryptopyrrole comes from *"kryptos,"* the Greek word
for "hidden," while "pyre" is a prefix for "fire." The deriva-

tion is both Greek and Latin, and pyrrole is a combination word meaning "fiery oil." Thus, kryptopyrrole becomes "hidden fiery oil," whose chemical structure resembles other chemicals known to be toxic to brain function, such as LSD.

The presence of kryptopyrrole in elevated amounts, although not considered a sign of a particular or specific disease entity, is considered a biochemical marker of psychiatric dysfunction, much like the reading of an elevated clinical thermometer. This biochemical metabolite (5 Hydroxy-kryptopyrrle Lactam) is normally present in humans in either very low amounts or not at all, and it can be detected in the urine, which may have a mauve-colored appearance.

Feeling now that he was finally on to something, the indefatigable Dr. Kraus studied even harder, and in doing so learned that any kryptopyrrole reading of 20mcg/100cc was cause for concern. Shawcross's readings were a massive ten times higher than this already incredible amount.

Kryptopyrrole is also related to bile, and when excessive amounts are present it can combine with vitamin B6 and zinc to cause a metabolic defect called "pyroluria." This proved to be another clue to understanding Shawcross, for pyrolurics function well in controlled settings of low stress, proper diet and predictability. Apart from the initial settling down periods, which are common to all prison inductees, Shawcross has always been quite at home within the structured prison system where he enjoys a balanced diet. Conversely, pyrolurics, such as Shawcross, appear to fare poorly outside of controlled conditions. Unable to control anger once provoked, they have mood swings, cannot tolerate sudden, loud noises, are sensitive to bright lights and tend to be "night" people. They usually skip breakfast, have trouble recalling night dreams and they suffer poor short-term memory, so they make bad liars. Sometimes, they lack pigment in the skin and are therefore pale. Their hair is prematurely grey and they have a diminished ability to handle stress. As such, they may be very dangerous and constitute a risk to the public—all of which matches Arthur identically.

All of this shows Shawcross's personality and behavior in an interesting light. Dr. Kraus argues that the symptoms manifested by Arthur Shawcross correlated in every way with one suffering from the abnormally elevated levels of this toxic chemical invasion. Parental disorientation, abnormal ECGs, general nervousness, progressive loss of ambition, poor school performance and decreased sexual potencies are all symptoms and all are embedded in this serial killer's personal history.

The abnormality also correlated with marked irritability, rages, inability to control anger once provoked, mood swings, terrible problems with stress control, violence and antisocial behavior, all aligned with the high risk of becoming violent that is evident in Arthur's behavior.

Mr. Shawcross was certainly born to kill—and then he learned to kill.

THE DOMINO EFFECT?

Faulty genes, an XYY chromosome disorder, kryptopyrrole (the "hidden fiery oil"), a wrongly "wired-up" hypothalamus—it appears each, or any combination of these, may lie as the root cause of antisocial behavior. As the recent study by the scientists at King's College London suggests, this may mean that we are spawning even more psychopaths and, therefore, breeding evil.

Perhaps there is a very strong argument to suggest that many of us are born to kill. Is there really a "demon seed" in our genes, our DNA or chromosomes? Science seems to be proving that this "demon seed" does exist. But even if it does, other external and social disorientations and adverse influences have to be in place before a fully-emerged serial killer explodes on society.

FBI HIGH RISK REGISTER

Of the thirteen "family background characteristics" the FBI have found to adversely affect a child's later behavior, the serial killer that fulfilled most of the criteria was Fred West. By the FBI's calculations, Fred West would have come very close to the top of their High Risk Register with a staggering score of 92.3 percent.

Fred would have checked these qualities off the list: psychiatric history, criminal history, sexual problems, physical abuse, psychological abuse and dominant father figure aligned with negative relationships with both his natural mother and father. He had been treated unfairly, had suffered head trauma. And because other members of his family—his mother, father, brother John and son Steven—all committed sex crimes, we may well assume that they all carried the demon seed.

In comparison with West, Donald "Pee Wee" Gaskins hit 100 percent. Henry Lee Lucas, one of the most notorious serial murderers in criminal history, also scores 100 percent. Aileen Wournos notches 84.5 percent, while Jeffrey Dahmer comes further down the "High Risk Register" at a mere 61.5 percent. Myra Hindley scored just 30.77 percent with Ian Brady at a surprisingly low 15 percent.

BORN TO KILL, BRED TO KILL, TAUGHT TO KILL, TRAINED TO KILL?

Theodore Robert Bundy "learned" to kill because he was bright and wanted to become a more competent hunter, just like all serial killers evolve and become proficient at what they do in order to be more effective and evade apprehension.

Those that are "trained" to kill are a different matter altogether. Unlike killers such as Ted Bundy, the initial choice to kill does not come from within but is stimulated by an external source such as a mentor, family member, friend or an institution such as the army. There are just two killers in this book that we can show to have been legally trained to kill, namely John Allen Muhammad and Dr. Harold Shipman. Muhammad was trained as a U.S. soldier to protect his country and kill if ordered to do so. Dr. Shipman enjoyed a medical education and on qualifying as a doctor swore by the Hippocratic Oath to care for the sick and save lives.

Serial killers, spree killers and mass murderers are the dark stars of modern culture. Luring victims to their death, they often act out extreme sadistic urges, and lack any ability to empathize with the suffering of their victims. Many of the faces in *How to Make a Serial Killer* are familiar, others are not, yet they all have one thing in common: They are all killers. Furthermore, they have all been extensively studied and analyzed: We know what they did and how they did it. By opening up the nature vs. nurture debate we now want to ask: What made them act that way? In *How to Make a Serial Killer* we investigate the paths these serial killers took from childhood to adulthood and uncover the factors that created these monsters of humanity.

As a basic guide, it seems that the entire serial killer's edifice is precariously balanced on pillars of denial, splitting, projection, rationalization and projective identification. Narcissistic injuries—life crises, such as abandonment, divorce, financial difficulties, incarceration and public opprobrium—can bring the whole thing tumbling down. The narcissist cannot afford to be rejected, spurned, insulted, hurt, resisted, criticized or disagreed with. Likewise, the serial killer is trying desperately to avoid a painful relationship with his object of desire. He is terrified of being abandoned or humiliated, exposed for what he is and then discarded.

This book contains fascinating testimony about the early years of these killers, investigates common patterns in their development and visits the scenes of their crimes. It gives information from investigating officers and TV and press coverage, which contributes to the efforts of professional profilers as they attempt to uncover the probable cause and effect that led these often normal children to turn into some of the most infamous killers the world has seen.

It is also interesting to note that similar early child-hood behaviors are common in most serial killers. According to Robert Ressler, an FBI profiler and author of several books including *Whoever Fights Monsters*, poten-tial killers become solidified in their loneliness from the ages of eight to twelve. "Such isolation is considered the single most important aspect of their psychological makeup," he writes, adding, "Loneliness and isolation do not always mean that the potential killers are introverted and shy; some are, but others are gregarious with other men, and are good talkers. The outward orientation of the latter masks their inner isolation." In addition, Ressler notes that of all the serial killers he has studied, at least 60 percent of them had wet the bed.

Each case study in this book follows the path of the individual from the cradle to—where applicable—the grave. We look at the parents, siblings, schooling and any form of mental and physical trauma they may have suf-fered—specifically head injuries—and other adverse fac-tors that might have turned normally ordinary children into monsters. We also examine each killer's psycho-pathology to discover if they all had low self-esteem and fragile egos. Without exception, they are all true socio-pathic personalities living in a world of self-denial—never at fault themselves. In their world, it is always someone else who is to blame.

CHAPTER 2

IVAN MILAT

*"I just can't begin to describe him as a human being.
I don't think that Milat had the feelings of a human
being."*

Ian Clarke, father of victim Caroline Clarke

AT THE TIME of his arrest, Ivan Milat was Australia's
worst serial killer. From 1989–1992 he abducted, robbed,
sexually molested, tortured and murdered seven backpackers and left their bodies in the Belanglo Forest, south
of Sydney. Did the harsh environment Milat grew up in
put him on the inevitable path to murder, or was he born
to kill?

Short, dark and wiry, with a penetrating gaze—all traits
he shared with Fred West—and sporting throughout his
killing years a thick "macho-man" moustache, Milat was
every inch the Australian Outback man. Hardy, indepen-

dent and self-sufficient: These were all qualities that served to make Milat a tough, ruthless loner who slaughtered his prey with a degree of sadism shocking even to those who study serial killers closely.

For many, Australia is a land promising adventure and excitement. Young people especially flock there from around the world, eager to explore its beaches, forests, deserts and wide open spaces. The Outback is a particular lure—a magical, mystical landscape that casts a spell on visitors. And it was here that Milat preyed on his victims, finding a steady stream of trusting young travelers to pick up on the lonely highways. Between 1989 and 1992, seven people (that we know of) were abducted in the Belanglo State Forest, which is situated in the Southern Tablelands, approximately 6 miles west of Moss Vale, just south of Sydney. An exotic pine forest, Belanglo boasts some impressive bush walking along its numerous trails. Bird watching is a favored activity at Belanglo.

But Milat had a different sort of activity in mind.

Until 1989, Australia enjoyed a reputation as one of the safest countries in the world. Some five million travelers journeyed there each year. By tradition, young backpackers would head for Sydney's student and travelers' district, Kings Cross, before setting off to explore the many natural wonders that Australia has to offer. Hitchhiking was a popular way of traveling around the vast country, and for a dangerous individual such as Milat, the prospect of so many young and vulnerable people wandering the roads and forests of his district was too great a temptation. Almost single-handedly, Ivan Milat would tarnish

Australia's reputation as a safe, welcoming place for independent travelers.

According to Commander Clive Small, a former Australian Police Superintendent, "He specifically targeted backpackers, because they were distant from relatives and friends. There was less likelihood of people knowing where they were or what they were doing." The treatment he subjected his victims to is almost unbelievable. As the forensic psychiatrist Dr. Rod Milton puts it, "Why he killed was shocking. Some people were tortured. Some people were sexually assaulted and killed. Some people were used as target practice. He was a man who enjoyed killing. He was a man who enjoyed the power and the sexual gratification that he got from his victims. I think it was violence for the sake of violence in someone who enjoyed the explosion of violence." Milat would sever his victims' spines in a deliberate effort to not only physically paralyze them, but to put them completely at his mercy. He would also bind his victims as he raped and abused them, before engaging in a final flurry of bloodletting as they were beaten and strangled, then stabbed and shot repeatedly. No one in Australia had ever seen anything like it.

Following the discovery of a double murder in Belanglo Forest, with graphic details of the slayings revealed to the public, it quickly became apparent that a sadistic murderer was on the loose, and that he was unlikely to stop killing any time soon.

These first two victims were a pair of nineteen-year-olds, James Gibson and Deborah Everist from Frankston,

Victoria. They were last seen alive on Friday, December 30, 1989 at Surrey Hills in Sydney, where they were planning to hitchhike the 87 miles to Albury.

The next victim followed soon after. Sunday, January 20, 1991, was the last day that twenty-year-old German backpacker Simone Schmidl was sighted in the town of Liverpool, west of Sydney. An intrepid girl known to her friends and family as "Simi," she had been hitchhiking south to meet her mother in Melbourne.

Twenty-one-year-old Gabor Kurt Neugebauer and his twenty-year-old girlfriend Anja Habschied were two more German hitchhikers out on their own. They left Sydney's Kings Cross district on December 20, 1991 to travel to Darwin. They never made it.

A British pair, Joanne Walters and Caroline Clarke, left Kings Cross on April 18, 1992. They had planned to travel around Australia, paying their way by picking fruit en route. Instead, like the rest of Milat's victims, their remains were later discovered in Belanglo State Forest.

Caroline's parents, Ian and Jacquie Clarke, remember being a little apprehensive before Caroline flew to Australia. Ian Clarke recalls, "Off she went, and she was having a wonderful time. You know, we always talked about hitchhiking as something that should not be encouraged. And we always said to Caroline, whatever you do, never do this on your own. Always use public transport, even if it meant working for a bit longer to pay for the fare. Well, she didn't." When Caroline went missing, her family did everything they could to search for her. They created fliers with Caroline's photograph and details on them and sent them to all the major backpacking hostels. Backpackers were asked to take bundles of posters with them and hand them out to other travelers. In this way, news of the missing girls quickly spread across the continent. However, despite Ian and Jacquie's best efforts, news was slow in coming through. It was a terrible time, as Jacquie explains, "You can't believe anything has gone wrong. But, of course you just can't believe it. However, as the weeks turned into months, the realization dawns. I was in a state of limbo, I must say." Her husband was equally traumatized, adding, "I don't think we really, until quite late on, finally faced up to the fact that they weren't coming back. Then a different kind of anguish comes in when you know they are dead. Then you can start to mourn them."

The Clarkes were able to begin to mourn their youngest daughter in September 1992. On the nineteenth, the remains of Joanne Walters were discovered under a rock in Belanglo. Her clothing, which lay nearby, had been carefully arranged, suggesting a sexual element to the crime. The following day, the body of Caroline Clarke was discovered by police just fifty feet away. The body was also left in a "posed" position, which clearly signified something to the killer. According to forensic psychiatrist Dr. Rod Milton, "She was lying face down, with one arm up and her head on her hand, and she had been repeatedly shot through the head. The autopsy reports show several entry points to the skull, which suggests that the killer had moved the head in order to do what pleased him. This was a particularly cold-blooded murder, although it is not unknown for serial killers to arrange the bodies in a particular way. There was some similarity between Miss Walters and Miss Clarke in that they were both laying face down, and both had their hands raised up somewhere near the vicinity of the head."

Once the Clarkes knew that their daughter had been murdered, they wanted to find out who did it. Ian Clarke says, "We knew the broad outline of what had happened to Caroline, and that was horrid because it was such an evil and disgusting event. You know, you start reliving it on their behalf, conjuring up what they'd gone through." Sadly for the Clarkes, it would be a while before the identity of their daughter's killer would be revealed.

The Hume Highway is the major arterial link between Sydney and Melbourne. The road travels for much of the way along the Great Dividing Range and passes through the Murray River towns of Albury and Wodonga. The Hume Highway was developed when paddle steamer trade along the river was the only way of marketing the crops and produce of the surrounding countryside. It passes near the Snowy Mountains, through the Riverina, Bushranger Country, and the Southern Highlands of New South Wales. It was along this same road that Milat picked up all of his victims for their final ride.

Ivan Milat, a trawler and opportunist—like so many serial murderers—would cruise the Hume on a regular basis. He was a hunter and this was his turf, the place he was most familiar with and where he was most comfortable in selecting his prey. The only other area where Milat felt as secure was the Belanglo State Forest, where he would take his victims to act out the final agonized stages of their lives.

Ivan's method of selecting his victims was very straightforward. When he spotted a likely victim or victims on the highway he would pull his blue, four-wheel drive vehicle over and start by offering a tried-and-tested cheery grin. He was adept at playing the role of the Good Samaritan, a friendly traveling companion. But once Ivan was sure his new traveling companions were safely in his control, things would quickly change. By the time his victims realized they were being kidnapped, it was too late. A gun would be pulled and his passengers would be tied up in quick order. Then it was off to the forest—Ivan's special place.

Milat enjoyed the isolation that the bush afforded him. Taking his victims to such a lonely setting was the perfect place for him to abuse them without fear of being disturbed. He could work in private, uninterrupted; he was a cold and selfish killer who could take all the time he desired with his immobilized victims. Like other such killers, he could control not only the manner of his victims' deaths, but what happened to them afterwards. He would play with the corpses of his victims, posing them in positions that held some secret meaning for him and then secreting the bodies in places and in a manner that would signify something intensely personal to him. He was following his own inner signature, lost in the compulsive pleasure that it lent him. Once he was satiated, Milat would strip the corpses of any jewelery or possessions he wished to retain and then, almost carelessly, hide the bodies beneath a makeshift blanket of branches and leaves.

There is something about Australia's serial killers that seems to separate them from the often diverse backgrounds of repetitive murderers from other countries. Australia's serial killers are almost exclusively from underprivileged backgrounds. They have poor work histories and nomadic tendencies. It is almost as if they are born outlaws who believe from the very beginning that they can and will do as they please. According to Paul Kidd, author of *Australian Serial Killers*, Milat exemplifies this attitude. He writes, "Milat was an extremely clever serial killer. I mean this within the Australian genre. By that I mean, it is a lonely place, it's in the bush and he is abducting strangers, people he doesn't know. He's taking them to a place of absolute isolation where he's committing his crimes... he is secreting the bodies, hiding the bodies, in a place where they are unlikely to be found. Ninety percent, or more probably, of Australia's serial killers, are pure opportunists."

Ivan was born on December 27, 1944, the fifth child in a family of fourteen. The Milat family lived in a very rural area, and so were a close-knit group. Suspicious of outsiders, they turned inwards and were bound together only by their loyalty to one another and their fierce family privacy. It is not difficult to imagine the Milat family as a hillbilly clan at large in the countryside.

One of the Milat family's favorite activities was gunplay. Ivan and his many brothers loved to mess around with guns—they even manufactured their own rifles and revolvers. Taking their weaponry, they would disappear into the forest to hunt rabbits and birds. Their father, Stephan, a Croatian immigrant, was a ruthless disciplinarian who thought nothing of beating his boys for any unruly behavior. The Milat children had an absolute fear of their father, and when they weren't working alongside him on the family's tomato crops they would generally try to escape his attentions altogether.

Stephen Milat was, of course, a product of a different time and culture. His neighbors recall one particularly disturbing incident of abuse involving Stephen standing upon the backs of two of his sons and beating them mercilessly with a piece of wood. Stephen's propensity for violence is well documented, and his sons regularly experienced it firsthand. However, rather than instill discipline, Stephan's punishments only created a bitter resentment in Ivan, who would grow to loathe authority in all its forms.

A significant point in Ivan's young life, and his first encounter with death, came when his sister Margaret was killed in a car accident. The accident happened close to the Milat family home and Ivan was able to race to the scene, where he found his own horribly injured sister in deep distress. Margaret was rushed to the hospital where she managed to hold on for two weeks before finally succumbing to her injuries, having never regained consciousness. The close-knit Milat family was devastated by its loss and Ivan, having witnessed some terrible scenes at the roadside, was hit the hardest.

The first effects of this trauma appeared when Ivan became a teenager. He began to retreat into an inner world and became obsessed with his own body. He would spend hours exercising and toning himself with weights. He dressed himself as expensively as his parents could afford and would pose with guns, as if living out some inner fantasy. All this far exceeded normal teenage vanity. Ivan was transfixed by his own appearance and his self-image assumed prime importance over everything else in his life. And beneath the rugged image he had created, the cauldron simmered. Ivan Milat was very angry at life. Perhaps he sensed that he was a born loser, too weak to break away from the family pack. Only his guns and bad-boy behavior seemed to give him some measure of relief.

Ivan would go shooting on his own sometimes, but more often than not, he would spend time with some of his brothers. Although they were a solid unit, at least one of Ivan's brothers began to harbor doubts about his behavior, especially his liking for guns. His younger brother George claimed, "Everybody in the family, a few of my brothers said 'well maybe there's something wrong with Ivan—there's definitely something wrong with him! Never leave a gun loaded, no matter what!'" As he slowly disengaged himself from the family unit, Milat became a petty criminal. Like Ian Brady, Ivan began to develop an idea of himself as a renegade and an outlaw.

Although Ivan wanted to join the big time criminal league, he never quite made it. But at the same time, his obsession with guns and his self-image as a renegade moved him away from the constraints of a society he had elected to go to war with. Neither professional criminal nor ordinary member of the public, Ivan existed in a kind of limbo. This made him a difficult person to be around, especially as he grew into a tough young man with a fiery temper when provoked and a highly developed inclination toward violence. "I didn't get along with Ivan because he was pretty wild. Maybe because I stayed out of trouble. He would fly off the handle at any chance, to the point that I wouldn't tell him anything anymore," said his brother George.

When he ventured outside of the family unit and tried to form human relationships with others, Ivan struggled. Peter Cantarella, who employed Ivan for one year at his fruit market, recalls that he initially saw Milat as a decent, hardworking young man. However, this impression did not last. Problems surfaced when Ivan asked Peter to become guarantor for a vehicle he wanted to purchase. Cantarella agreed, on the understanding that the loan Ivan needed to buy the car would be repaid. Ivan bought the car and then defaulted on the loan, leaving Cantarella liable for it. At first, Ivan went underground, but when he did finally resurface it wasn't to ask Cantarella for forgiveness. Instead, with his brothers in tow, Ivan began to harass Cantarella and his wife. The situation steadily worsened as the Milats stole guns and jewelry from Cantarella and his wife, then they would turn up at the Cantarella family home and pelt it with stones. A no-nonsense character himself, Cantarella decided to take matters in his own hands when Ivan and his family showed up one day, brandishing their weapons and threatening robbery. He remembers, "Milat walked into my shop with his brothers and guns, and took the jewelry off my first wife, and I thumped him in the head. He was just getting in the wrong crowd and it was getting bad."

Ivan's car trouble marked the beginning of his life outside the law. Along with some of his brothers, Ivan embarked on a crime spree, robbing and vandalizing his way through town. The Milat boys were troublemakers but were hardly master criminals. Although they were always in trouble with the law, the Milat's crimes were not the kind to bring them national notoriety. Ivan seems to have been an especially inept villain. He began with stealing cars and burglary, and one day graduated on to breaking into an army barracks and making off with a safe.

But Milat was not what one could call an effective criminal. More often than not, he was caught and incarcerated. Once in prison he was able to mix with other criminals, some of them men who were truly evil and psychopathic. The type of men who, like Ivan, held a grudge against society and who at the same time felt they were being persecuted by it.

In 1971, not long after being discharged from his most recent stint in jail, Ivan Milat committed an act which instantly took him from the ranks of small-time crooks and put him into a much higher league. He decided to abduct two female hitchhikers who were on their way to Melbourne. In what would become his hallmark, Milat picked up the two young women in an initially friendly manner and quickly metamorphosed into a monster once he had them under his control. When the girls realized the danger they were in, they played a successful psychological game with Milat. He had made it clear that he intended to kill both women, so one of them struck a bargain with Milat—that he should let them live if she agreed to have sex with him. Shortly after Milat released his two captives, he found himself arrested and charged with rape (the charge was later dropped when one of the victims changed her testimony).

Despite the fact that he had ultimately been acquitted, the message was clear to Ivan Milat: If he let his victims live, they would run and tell their tales. It would be better for Milat if they died. By killing them it also meant he could take his time with them, do exactly as he pleased and have as much "fun" as he wanted. And why not? They would be dead at the end of it anyway, he reasoned.

At this stage in his development Milat was still the anger-fueled, resentful and fractious child he had always been. To project the desired self-image he had painstakingly prepared for himself, Milat would abstain from drinking and drug-taking, signaling him out as very different from other people of his age and social situation at the time. Once again we see parallels with Fred West, who was quite happy to watch others lose control while under the influence of alcohol, but who himself remained rigidly in control. It heightened his sense of superiority over those around him. There is no reason to think any differently about the attitude of Ivan Milat. This compulsive quality is something he would later extend to his own home and property. As with many other organized serial killers, John Gacy being pre-eminent among them, Milat would have to keep his property immaculate at all times. This is a classic displacement activity—a way of controlling one's own environment when someone is not necessarily able to take charge of other areas of their personal life.

At the age of thirty, Ivan Milat met a girl named Karen Duck. She was six months pregnant with another man's child and, needing someone who would be prepared to care for her and her unborn child, she agreed to stay with Milat. There is no indication that Karen ever loved Ivan— or indeed that he loved her—but he eventually asked her to marry him and she agreed. The relationship was doomed from the outset.

Karen soon discovered that Ivan was incredibly domineering and jealous. He would often not even allow her to leave the house. When he did, he would demand that she tell him exactly where she had been and what she had been doing while she was away from his watchful gaze. He also forced Karen to account for every cent that she spent, and demanded to see receipts for everything she bought. Karen would later recount the way her husband was able to control his emotions, the same way he did with other aspects of his life and surroundings. Rather than burst into frequent fits of rage, Milat would smoulder quietly instead. When he did lose his temper, his rage was all the more fearsome for it.

The marriage inevitably came to an end. Karen had been so thoroughly demeaned and beaten down by her husband that she couldn't stand it anymore. The specter of violence had loomed over their entire relationship, and it was a brave and difficult decision to make on Karen's part. Naturally, Milat was furious at his wife's rejection and was typically unable to accept any part of the blame for the failure of his marriage. After brooding on his marital breakdown for a while, Milat's rage finally exploded and he took his revenge by setting fire to Karen's parents' house. George Milat says of his brother's actions, "He was upset about the divorce... and what I know of... he caused it. He started punching [Karen] and the police were called. When Ivan got violent, he got very violent."

When Karen left Ivan, he lost the one person he was able to utterly control, the person who allowed him to walk all over her and vent his frustrations at life. Now, with her gone, there was just the hopeless inadequate Ivan, left once again to his own devices. There was no one to take it all out on anymore.

One theory about Milat argues that it was his marital breakdown that caused him to exercise his fantasies about power and domination on the Hume Highway. While this idea is certainly in part valid, it is also the case that Ivan already harbored deeply entrenched dreams of depravity, even before his marriage. It is highly unlikely that this single event, as emotionally damaging as it was, was the sole reason Milat finally felt the urge to go out seeking victims to murder. It may have triggered the mechanism that turned him into a killer, but all the ingredients were firmly in place long before that.

On July 13, 1989, Karen and Ivan Milat divorced. Six months later, the first two of his victims would die.

As much as guns held his fascination as a boy, as he grew up, Ivan's love for them strengthened even more. Milat had become a man accustomed to believing himself above the scrutiny of society and the law. His vast arsenal of weapons reinforced the outlaw image he coveted. Growing up, he and his brothers had even constructed their own shooting range on the family property. Photographs taken of Ivan, from boy to man, show a smiling, triumphant individual, small but big-muscled, cradling his guns the way another man might hold a girlfriend. His weapons were very important to him. So much so that he could not even resist taking some of them to his job working on the roads.

Ivan's boss at the time, Don Borthwick, remembered him well. "You have the drinkers and the players. But Ivan had a knife... you could have cut up a horse with that knife." Borthwick also remembers that Ivan was never really the kind of man to socialize with his workmates, preferring to sit quietly with a book and a soft drink while his co-workers drank beer and engaged in the usual sort of barroom bravado. Nor did he chase after women, as many of his co-workers did. Ivan Milat was content to go straight home after work and lose himself in one of his gun magazines. He was a very private man.

Borthwick also told of the occasions when Milat would proudly display his gun collection for the guys. He would grin broadly as everyone made a fuss over the impressive weapons, just as though he were a father showing off his newborn child. And then there was the large Bowie knife that Milat always carried. He claimed to use it for cutting up apples, but Borthwick told him he thought it would be better for cutting up animals. Milat merely laughed at this and said something about how you could never be too careful and that you never knew who was watching.

On Thursday, January 25, 1990, when he was sure no one was watching, Ivan Milat went out cruising the Hume Highway, where he picked up Paul Onions, an English backpacker. Unlike Milat's first two victims, Onions was able to escape before Milat was able to secure him. One can only imagine the fate that would have befallen him had he not. Milat had spotted Paul at a newsstand beside the highway and offered him a lift. Paul accepted and the pair hopped into Milat's truck. As the journey progressed, Paul's perception of the driver altered. As with Caroline Owens, who found herself at the mercy of Fred and Rose West after being picked up by them at the side of the road, Onions felt a pronounced change in atmosphere once he was inside the vehicle. Where Fred West had at this point stopped the car and punched Caroline in the face to subdue her, Ivan Milat pulled over and produced a pistol. Clearly in big trouble, Onions made the split-second decision that saved his life: He leapt from the vehicle and ran.

Zigzagging along the highway as he had been taught by the navy to avoid gunfire, Onions managed to evade the shots that Milat fired at him. Onions managed to flag down a passing car and Milat jumped back into his vehicle and sped away. While the likes of Ted Bundy would have been back out searching for a victim later that same night, Milat, opportunistic and driven sexual murderer though he was, demonstrated remarkable restraint. It would be another year before he would launch another attack.

Onions, badly shaken by his ordeal, gave a statement to detectives that was dutifully filed away. Though he had obviously had a brush with death, the detectives dealing with Onions' case did not take things any further. At the time it seemed like a one-time attack. Four years and several murders later, the assault on Paul Onions would take on a grim significance.

As a serial killer, the level of sadism that Ivan Milat exhibited in his murders escalated radically as the killings progressed. There is evidence of sexual assaults committed on both his male and female victims, and there was an evident satisfaction in placing them in restraints and molesting one victim before the horrified eyes of another. This high degree of humiliation was vital to Milat's fantasies of dominance and control. He reveled in placing his victims in tight, inescapable bondage and as with Fred West delighted in subjecting them to the most cruel of tortures before finally dispatching them.

Victims would typically be tied up with rope, elaborately gagged with cloth and stabbed in the spine to paralyze and humble them even more. The gag was most likely a crucial part of Milat's signature, because it contributed to his ultimate goal of the complete dehumanization of his victims. Unable to speak or communicate intelligibly, his victims were rapidly stripped of their personalities. This would be of prime importance to a control freak such as Milat.

Some victims also had their faces obscured with articles of their own clothing during the attacks. They were blind and muted as their sadistic assailant hacked and stabbed at them. This would have thrilled Milat even more. He was a killer who experimented with different methods of dispatching his victims. Some were beaten, some were strangled. Others were shot and stabbed. Multiple knife wounds were often inflicted on his prey in a methodical or detailed pattern. This is a demonstration of the killer's "picquerism" (a term used to classify a sexually deviant condition in which the offender harbors an unhealthy predilection for using a knife to penetrate or cut a person).

The savagery of these murders was part of a steadily evolving ritual. The more Milat killed, the more ferocious the assaults became. Anja Habschied, her hands tied behind her, was made to kneel down as if at a public execution before being beheaded with a sword. Other victims were stabbed and slashed around the face and head. Many cases demonstrated instances of extreme "overkill," demonstrating Milat's almost unfathomable level of hatred for his victims. Some had been frenziedly stabbed, then shot multiple times in the head. In a number of cases, the head wounds were deliberately arranged to expose different areas of the skull to further attack. The aim was clearly to destroy, and each act was a different phase along an arc of pure sadism, committed out of an intense desire to inflict maximum suffering on a bound and helpless human being. Milat, as with so many other sexually sadistic serial killers, was a compulsive trophy taker, hoarding items of clothing and other personal effects as souvenirs that he could utilize later to relive his horrible deeds.

Seven murders and a forest full of death proved to be the undoing of Ivan Milat. When it became obvious that a demented serial killer was at work, the police went all out to catch their man. It did not take long for the Milat family to come under suspicion. As a family already well-known to the police and the authorities, it was only a matter of time before the male members of the clan would come under official scrutiny. It was certainly a fact that several Milat brothers matched at least some of the profiles put together to describe the Belanglo Forest murderer. In the event, most turned out to have solid alibis. The exception was Ivan Milat, and he was placed under surveillance. Later examination of his and other family members' homes yielded a wealth of evidence in the form of victims' personal property. Forensic links were also established.

After months of close surveillance, the police finally secured a search warrant and raided Milat's home on May 22, 1994. Neil Mercer from *The Sunday Telegraph* closely followed the case. "When the police raided the house, they found a treasure trove of evidence. There were backpacks, there were tents, there were cooking sets that had belonged to some of the backpackers. There were cameras, there were all sorts of things that could be traced back to individual backpackers." These items would later provide much of the evidence to convict Milat.

Police also raided the houses of other members of the Milat family. They found a huge amount of ammunition, an arsenal of weapons, and rope and cable ties that were identical to those found at the murder scenes. The Crown Prosecutor Mark Tedeschi explains that there was even more convincing evidence:

There was some rope found in a pillowcase at Milat's home. There was some blood on this rope, and this blood was analyzed and DNA profiling linked it to Mr. and Mrs. Clarke. Police found parts of a gun hidden in a wall cavity in Milat's home. Ballistic tests proved that it was one of two weapons used in two of the murders. Milat's response was, "I know nothing about the weapon," even though it was painted with camouflage paint, and there were a whole load of other weapons that he acknowledged were his painted in exactly the same camouflage paint.

One item that Milat didn't hide was a framed photograph of his girlfriend wearing a distinctive Benetton top. It was the same top that had been owned by Caroline Clarke.

More than ten years after Milat's arrest, Police Superintendent Clive Small, who headed the task force set up to deal with the backpacker murders, spoke about his thoughts on Milat. Superintendent Small observed that Milat's serial killer signature revealed "a pattern of behavior that goes clearly beyond just the killing of a person, and continues well after."

As with the Russian cannibal Andrei Chikatilo—responsible for at least fifty-two brutal slayings—Ivan Milat felt compelled to hurt and terrorize his victims as much as possible. Both men preferred the outdoors as locations to perpetrate their killings, favoring dense woodland—a private place where they could spend a lot of time undisturbed with their victims. Some killers return to the scene of an undiscovered body to gloat, masturbate or even engage in sexual acts with a decaying corpse. There is every reason to expect that Milat had returned to his own personal graveyard.

Using gags to muffle his captives' pain, Milat would delight in maiming them with his weapons. While Chikatilo relished hearing his child victims' screams whenever possible, Milat actually enjoyed gagging his. It furthered the control element to his fantasies as well as having the practical advantage of quieting their agonized cries. Evident in Milat's case, too, as with Bundy, Gacy and Dean Corll amongst so many others, is a unique thrill gleaned from committing double homicides. Having a terrified boyfriend watch helplessly as his girl-friend was assaulted and killed, and vice versa, gave Milat insurmountable pleasure.

It has been alleged by one of Milat's brothers that Ivan may have been responsible for up to twenty-eight mur-ders, and that he also confessed the crimes to his mother, who has since passed away. Ivan was proven to have had an opportunity to commit the crimes associated with them each and every time.

Ivan Milat was arrogant and macho—a classic bully–loser type with a gargantuan chip on his shoulder. He was someone who craved attention, even if it was only in the form of notoriety. In prison for the rest of his days, he was moved to a maximum-security jail after a failed escape attempt. Milat, the tough guy, is segregated from many of his fellow inmates for his own protection. He has bragged that if ever presented with the opportunity, he will escape from prison. He has also never once publicly admitted culpability for any of the murders.

Nevertheless, it is our opinion, based on viewing hours of trial testimony and reviewing the evidence in this case, that Milat's guilt in these homicides is beyond reasonable doubt. Though the science of psychological profiling is far from the gospel truth, Milat's profiles closely resemble those based on the Belanglo killer. This, coupled with the rest of the police and prosecution's findings, makes for a strong case indeed. Milat's insistence that he is innocent is common among serial killers, especially seasoned and psychopathic criminals like him.

For the families of the victims, Milat's utter lack of remorse is yet another callous blow. Talking about their daughter Caroline, Jacquie and Ian Clarke remember fondly their bright and bubbly girl who had always dreamed of visiting Australia. She was a wilful, adventurous spirit, always keen to explore. When her wish was eventually granted, only to be cut dreadfully short by a pathetic, anger-driven, sexually inadequate monster, the pain was almost too much for her parents to bear. "I couldn't bring myself to believe that such an insignificant little man could have wrought such horror and misery on so many people," says Ian Clarke. All these years later, the agony of knowing exactly what happened to their daughter is still very much with the couple, though they remained admirably composed during our interview with them. Resolute and dignified, they will not allow their daughter's killer the satisfaction of seeing their own destruction.

Ian recalls the occasion as he sat in court at Milat's murder trial when the wilting defendant, now lacking his trademark moustache, slipped up under clever questioning about a pair of gloves worn during some of the murders. Milat, under pressure had yelled, "I never wore any...," before stopping himself.

"You could have heard a pin drop. It was a magical moment," recalls Ian Clarke. Though the physical and circumstantial evidence against Milat was already more than clear, Ian Clarke knew then that Milat was indeed Caroline's killer. Though emotional, he was jubilant, knowing in his heart that the police had the right man and that he would pay for what he had done to Caroline and the others.

Ultimately, even members of Milat's own family turned against him. The words of his brother George testify to that: "I think he was more than twisted... he was definitively gone. Some of my brothers said there must be something wrong with him. Something wrong with him? Of course there was something wrong with him. The jail he's in? It's a special prison within a prison. What's he going to do there? I don't really know... I don't really care. It's his fault for landing in there. He's been in trouble all his life." Milat's lawyer Terry Martin explains, however, that Ivan still maintains his innocence no matter what: "My client's instructions to me were that he did not do it. Therefore, if he didn't do it, then someone terribly close to him must have. [But] when he spoke at his trial, he didn't do himself any favors at all." Milat's protestations of innocence, however callous, still find an audience willing to listen to him, but Neil Mercer of *The Sunday Telegraph* sums up the Milat case best of all. "There are the occasional outbreaks of 'Milat is innocent,' but I think that's garbage. If you look at all the evidence, read the trial transcript, look at the exhibits and where they were found, and Milat's answers in court—there is no doubt that he killed those seven people.

FBI HIGH RISK REGISTER—IVAN MILAT

1.   Alcohol abuse
2.   Drug abuse
3.   Psychiatric history

4. Criminal history
5. Sexual problems
6. Physical abuse
7. Psychological abuse
8/9. Dominant father figure aligned with a negative relationship with male caretaker figures
10. Negative relationships with both natural mother and or adoptive mother
11. Treated unfairly
12. Head trauma
13. Demon seed

1	2	3	4	5	6	7	8/9	10	11	12	13	%
0	0	0	X	X	X	X	XX	0	X	0	X	77

CHAPTER 3

FRED AND ROSE WEST

*"[Fred West] was a man devoid of compassion, con-
sumed with sexual lust, a sadistic killer and someone who had opted out of the human race... the very
epitome of evil."*

Richard Ferguson, prosecuting
lawyer at the trial of Rosemary West.

CROMWELL STREET IS not one of Gloucester's most
desirable areas. While this is certainly true now, it was
still the case even before the horrors that unfolded there
were revealed in 1994. The late-Victorian properties that
made up the street had long been in decline, with many
of them converted from family homes into flats and bed-
sits housing a rootless population of short-term tenants.

Crime was an issue around Cromwell Street. Needless to say, it was not the best place to live in Gloucester.

25 Cromwell Street was a three-story, semi-detached house covered in unexciting cookie-colored cladding—the sort of house you wouldn't take a second look at. Even if the outside of the house was dull, events inside were anything but. Its owner was a construction worker who was always at work making improvements to the property—knocking down a wall here, concreting over a floor there. To the casual observer, there always seemed to be something going on inside 25 Cromwell Street.

The house was owned by Fred West, and most people liked him. In the words of the journalist Hugh Worsnip "If you passed Fred West in the street, you wouldn't give him a passing glance. He had a wife and six children."

Always keen to help out, Fred was the local area's Mr. Fixit. If you had a leaky faucet or a loose roof tile, Fred would fix it for you. No job was too small and nothing was too much trouble for him. He always wore a cheery grin and had a ready "good morning" for his neighbors. Though he was not a big man, just 5 feet 6 inches, Fred was nevertheless a strong man, with powerful shoulders and arms earned after a lifetime's hard labor. Looking at Fred in the street, one could have imagined that this little man was locked in a 1970s time warp, with his thick mutton-chop sideburns and unruly mop of curly, dark hair. He was swarthy, too, looking like the stereotypical slippery fairground worker with a ready, gap-toothed smile, broken nose and piercing blue eyes that never missed a trick.

He loved to chat as well. Always talking, Fred's bub-
bling, manic personality was a stark contrast to that of
his dumpy, plain-looking wife Rosemary, who never had
much to say for herself as she walked with her children
down the street. Occasionally, she would yell at the kids
and pinch their ears for some transgression or other. But
it was Fred who was the chatterbox, even if he got carried
away with himself and his dialogue became a little too
sexually orientated and smutty, which it was prone to. It
was just Fred being Fred. He was the man that everybody
knew and liked. "He was very much a completely ordinary handyman and construction worker who got along
well with everybody," says journalist Dave Newman.
Good old Fred, with his constant supply of roll-up ciga-
rettes and his work jacket. A real character, in fact.

The sight of police cars on Cromwell Street was nothing unusual, but when the patrol vehicles pulled up outside 25 Cromwell Street on February 24, 1994, there was
more than a stir of interest among the locals. It was
clearly "not the usual domestic disturbance," as one
neighbor put it. With the benefit of hindsight, residents
today recall more than the usual curtain-twitching taking place. The more dramatically inclined residents
painted a picture of a pregnant gloom falling over the
street as the police rolled up and four grim-faced officers
entered the house. Whatever the atmosphere was like on
that day—real or imagined—it was a fateful event for
everyone concerned, and one that would reveal Fred
West to be one of the most evil monsters that Britain has
ever produced.

It was the heavily bespectacled Rosemary West, twelve years her husband's junior, who opened the door to the police and found herself squinting at a search warrant which, as the officers informed her, entitled them to dig up her backyard. After a moment's pause, she called back into the house for someone to find Fred. This was serious. Stephen West, Fred and Rose's nineteen-year-old son, reached his father on his mobile phone. Fred was spraying attic timbers for woodworm at a house in Stroud. When the youth told him that the police were at their home about to dig up the backyard, Fred listened calmly and responded that all would be fine. He would leave his job at once and be home soon.

Had Fred West gone straight home, he would have been back at Cromwell Street within thirty minutes, but he had a few other tasks to attend to first. Once he'd dealt with these, he could go home, confront the police and explain about Heather—because that was the name of the girl they were looking for. She was his daughter.

Fred West walked in through his front door more than four hours later. For once he didn't bustle in with his usual gruff greeting and chipper yet tuneless whistling. Something was obviously on his mind. The four officers had gone by this time, although they had left a policeman standing guard at the back of the house. Whatever was happening, Fred was not out of the woods yet.

Fred's first port of call was the cupboard under the stairs. He had been illegally rerouting electricity for years and was enjoying very low utility bills as a result. It was a clumsy operation involving a coat hanger and a bit of dangerous rewiring that could have easily electrocuted

Fred if it had not been done correctly. This type of low-level con was typical of West, a cocky guy who would help himself to anything that wasn't nailed down and who would rely on a bit of rough-hewn charm if caught in the act. He was a scavenger and a hoarder, a bit of a wheeler-dealer. In this instance he seemed very concerned that the policeman in the backyard would discover his meter scam, but he didn't seem overly bothered about anything else. After covering up his understairs electricity meter, Fred took Rose aside and conferred with her in hushed tones and whispers. Then the pair disappeared upstairs to talk further. When an outwardly cool Fred reemerged into the living room it was to announce to his family that he was going to the police station to make a statement.

When he arrived at the police station, Fred indignantly claimed that the "Old Bill" (UK slang for "cops") were harassing him because of an earlier prosecution of rape against him which had failed because of lack of evidence. The police were pursuing a vendetta against him, he claimed. No, he was told. This time the potential charge was much more serious. The police were in fact trying to establish whether Fred West had murdered his daughter Heather.

She had disappeared seven years previously, sometime in June. It was "nonsense," Fred told detective Hazel Savage. He had been visited only recently by his daughter, when he was on remand at Winson Green Prison in Birmingham. He still saw Heather occasionally and had recently lunched with her in Devizes, Wiltshire. She was into drugs now, he explained, and was not on the best of terms with her family. This was the reason why she no longer lived at the family home. Fred told Detective Savage that he still had a soft spot for his daughter and arranged to meet her clandestinely, so as not to alert Rose who wanted nothing more to do with her.

Detective Savage was not convinced. Instead, she put it bluntly to West that she suspected that he had murdered his daughter and had buried her somewhere on his property—under the patio, to be precise. "I think we'd best stop this, don't you Hazel? We're talking nonsense here," Fred argued. He left the police station under the cover of darkness, having not been charged, and returned to spend his last night of freedom at home.

Early the next morning, the searchers returned to carry on their excavations in the West family backyard. Stephen West, on his way to work, happened to pass by his father, who was standing at an upstairs window as if mesmerized and was gazing down upon the police diggers in his backyard. Stephen later recalled that his father had slowly turned to him, "and his eyes bore straight through me." Stephen was shaken by the blank, muddy stare he had drawn from Fred. It was a look he had never seen from his father before. It was the look of a knowing evil that had come to the end of its reign.

The game was up for Fred West, and he knew it. Now it was a case of protecting his wife and minimizing the damage. When Hazel Savage arrived at the home that morning to charge Frederick West with murder, he explained that he was willing to accompany them to the station. There was something he wanted to get off his chest, he said. On his way out to a waiting police

car, for the evident benefit of his neighbors and a smat-
tering of local reporters, he yelled that he had nothing
to do with Heather's disappearance and that he certainly had not murdered her. Then, as he climbed into the
police car beside Detective Savage, he said to her in a
quiet voice, "I killed her."

As the police and the world would soon discover, Fred
West really had killed his daughter—and she was not his
only victim. As it turned out, there was a lot more to this
seemingly happy-go-lucky construction worker than met
the eye.

At Gloucester Police Station, West told the investigating officers where Heather's body was buried. He seemed
particularly helpful but was overly concerned that the
police confine their digging just to the area of the backyard that he had directed them to. Fred told them that
she lay beneath the paved floor of his patio, between a
stand of fir trees and the side of the adjoining Seventh
Day Adventist Church. Keep digging, he told them, and
you will find her soon enough. He also mentioned that if
they dug deep enough they would come across an
ancient stream that flowed below his backyard. This last
revelation gave Detective Savage pause for thought. How
could Fred know about the stream unless he had dug
down that far himself?

The diggers began their search where Fred told them to,
but also began to search other parts of the garden, just in
case Heather wasn't where she was supposed to be. As
they did this, the already grim search became much
worse. As the pathologist Professor Bernard Knight
recalls, "I still remember Detective Superintendent John

Bennett's face when I went down into the hole in the backyard, and I looked up and said that either you've got more than one, or she's got three legs, because here's another two thigh bones. From then on we just found more and more. This was no big deal for me, but the police were dumbstruck." When confronted with the evidence that there was more than one body buried in his backyard Fred hung his head and muttered, "That's Shirley. The one who caused all the trouble."

On February 26, scene-of-the-crime officers removed from the backyard the dismembered remains of eighteen-year-old Shirley Robinson, a one-time lodger with the Wests who had vanished in 1978. They also exhumed the remains of Alison Chambers, a sixteen-year-old who had disappeared from a Gloucester children's home in August 1979. Finally, of course, they also discovered the skeleton of Heather West, also sixteen, missing since 1987. Police had now found three corpses in Fred West's backyard, and he had a lot of explaining to do.

And explain he did. To the investigating officers' shock and horror, West told them in matter-of-fact detail how he had strangled Heather to death during an argument about her wanting to leave home, and then began to dismember her body. "I remember it made a heck of a noise when it was breaking, a horrible noise, like scrunching, I suppose," he explained as he gave them the details of how he had removed his own daughter's head by sawing and twisting it off. He then cut off both her legs and dumped her in a wheelbarrow for later disposal. All of this was recounted in a flat, bland monotone by an impassive West. The officers had to quickly come to terms with the fact that they were not dealing with an ordinary domestic homicide. It very soon became apparent that the middle-aged man they were talking to was a psychopath, and one who had been committing terrible atrocities for so long that he had forgotten what normal human emotions were—if he ever had any in the first place. His confessions, with all their bloodless detachment, were the outpourings of a captured and stunned beast.

These revelations came just hours into the inquiry. Few could have guessed even then just how far into the abyss Frederick West had cast himself.

When it became obvious that the entire property would need to be searched thoroughly, officers relocated to the West's basement. By the end of the first week of March, they had discovered six more of Fred West's homicidal secrets. The bodies they found all belonged to girls that had been missing since the early 1970s. Some of the missing girls had been the subjects of massive police hunts. Pathologist Professor Bernard Knight remembers the scene: "In the cellar, Fred had put down a thick layer of concrete on top of a polythene membrane, because the River Severn flooded now and again and the cellar filled up with water. The police had to drill all the cement out and start hacking away at the mud, which was pretty foul stuff because Fred had also broken the sewer pipe, so it was mixture of mud and sewage... I had to go down the holes to recover whatever was there."

Twenty-one-year-old Lucy Partington, a niece of novelist Kingsley Amis, went missing from Cheltenham two days after Christmas in 1973. Despite televised appeals from her family followed by intensive searches, she would be not be found until police began digging in Fred West's basement some twenty years later. In one subsequent confession, when Fred West wasn't demeaning his victims yet further by spreading the cruel falsehood that his victims had all been in love with him and had accompanied him voluntarily, West revealed that Lucy had actually been kidnapped from a bus stop outside Cheltenham's Pittville Park. As the search for the missing university student got underway, Lucy was held captive, bound and gagged at 25 Cromwell Street. There is some evidence that she was kept alive in that dark, nightmarish cellar for almost a week as she was repeatedly tortured and sexually violated. After death, her body was sliced into pieces and dumped in a narrow, 3-foot shaft beneath the then-earthen floor.

The others that were found had all met similar fates. Lynda Gough, nineteen, the first known Cromwell Street victim, had known the Wests and had been a frequent visitor to their home. Some time in April 1973 she became a captive in their home. She would have been subjected to horrendous torture and sexual abuse, from possibly both Fred and Rose. Bindings were found in Lynda's makeshift tomb, as they were with all the other dead girls. Bondage, by now, seemed to be a consistent theme within the West's atrocities. They preferred their young victims tied up and helpless. Ropes, plastic harnesses, ligatures fashioned from the victims' clothing, masking tape gags—all were present in these awful death holes.

On November 10, 1973, fifteen-year-old Carol Ann Cooper set off for a night out at the movies. She was never seen again and, like the others, was later found buried beneath Fred West's cellar floor. The same fate awaited twenty-one-year-old Swiss student Therese Siegenthaler, who never arrived in Ireland, to where she had been hitchhiking. She was last seen on April 15, 1974. When police dug her up from the cellar of 25 Cromwell Street on March 5, she too had been reduced to a chopped up pile of bones.

The last time fifteen-year-old Shirley Hubbard was seen alive was November 14, 1974. The discovery of her remains was perhaps one of the most horrific of all. The young girl's skull was found to be completely encased in masking tape. She had not been able to see, speak or hear as her captors acted out their depraved fantasies upon her tightly bound body. Investigators even discovered a couple of small sections of plastic tubing, which had been inserted into the victim's nostrils so that she would be able to breathe and endure whatever sickening assaults the Wests inflicted on her restricted body.

Juanta Mott was seventeen years old when she vanished. She, like Lynda Gough before her, knew the Wests very well and had stayed at 25 Cromwell Street for some time. On April 12, 1975, she was due to babysit for a couple of friends she was staying with. She had been out earlier in the day and never returned. She had been bound, raped, tortured, killed and dumped in the West's basement.

After confessing to the murders at Cromwell Street, Fred West then stunned his interrogators by admitting to even more homicides away from this address. He also, he revealed, murdered his former wife, a girlfriend and his step-daughter. He directed police investigators to his former residence at 25 Midland Road, Gloucester, as well as to two fields close to his boyhood home in Herefordshire. On Monday, April 11, 1994, at Letterbox Field in Much Marcle where Fred had grown up, police found the remains of West's first wife, twenty-six-year-old Rena Costello. Like all the rest, she had been dismembered and packed into a small hole in the earth. The following month, on May 5, the body of eight-year-old Charmaine West was exhumed from beneath the concrete floor of Midland Road. Finally, on June 7, the corpse of nineteen-year-old Anne McFall was unearthed from Fingerpost Field in Much Marcle. These new burial grounds—at Fred's old house and at sites close to his boyhood home—were deeply significant. They were the tell tale signs of an obsessive serial killer, the type of man who exhibits the need to keep "his" girls under complete control, even after death.

As West began to confess, he began to lie even more than his usual. As his bizarre mental tapestry began to unravel and his sanity appeared to plummet, his explanations for the girls' fates became all the more outrageous. They were all in love with him, he claimed. They had threatened to tell his wife about their affairs with him. They all were into bondage and sado-masochism and had strangled or hung themselves by accident as they dangled from the rafters of his cellar, or choked on ropes cinched about their necks. It was "enjoyment that turned to disaster," said Fred. It was all a complete pack of lies.

The unfortunate girls that found themselves in the clutches of Fred West and, allegedly, his wife were at the mercy of a sadistic psychopathy so abhorrent as to be entirely off the scale of human understanding. It was almost as if they were in Hell. Twelve victims, all hideously mutilated and destroyed, and for what? The answers are both complex and oddly simple. A mixture of depravity and necessity. The thing to bear in mind when dealing with someone such as Fred West is that he is the type of person who does not recognize the social conventions that most of us adhere to and who does not accept traditional morality or codes of behavior.

In some cases, Fred described the murders as acts of necessity. After all, having kidnapped and abused his victims so terribly, the only logical thing Fred could do to them to avoid capture was kill them. But for the most part, his reasons for what he did sprang from his need to fulfill an alien desire that had developed within him, a need to satisfy some form of perverse sexual desire. He craved the dark excitement his deeds offered to him, and each attack became a progressively worse abomination. As his attacks gathered momentum, Fred West entered into a downward spiral of total depravity and became an utterly unhinged sexual deviant. He would not stop unless he was stopped.

Fred West was born in the small, rural village of Much Marcle, Herefordshire, England, on September 29, 1941, and from day one he was doomed. Descending from a long line of countrymen on both sides of his family, he would be raised to follow traditional West Country ways. However, small village life was not all crop harvesting and cider-making. It had its dark side, too, and Fred was exposed to it from the earliest age, leaving its indelible mark on him forever.

Early photographs of the infant Fred reveal a somewhat focused-looking child with distinctive luminescent eyes. At the time he had a full head of curly blond hair, which would later darken.

Fred's father, Walter West, was the man whose seed created a demon. A cowman, Walter was some years older than his maidservant wife, Daisy, who was just sixteen when they married. Hard farm labor was what Walter did, and he expected his eldest son to follow in his footsteps. He also expected other things from his child that no son should ever be expected to give.

Freddy was not an only child. As the years went by, Walter and Daisy produced six more siblings. Fred had little time for his brothers and sisters, except the second eldest, John, who was a fairly tough youngster and whom Freddy relied upon throughout his youth to get him out of the various scrapes he got into because of his big mouth. The brothers were close—close enough for one of Fred's daughters to later reveal that both Fred and John, along with their father Walter, had repeatedly raped her over a number of years.

Fred West was no scholar. He could not spell and had difficulty writing. However, none of this mattered to him because he knew how to talk. Fred West had the gift of the gab and could think on his feet. In sleepy, rural Herefordshire, where life moved at a sedate pace and where academic qualifications were less valued than an aptitude for hard work, Fred got by just fine. Country folklore had it that work was what life was all about—and hard work at that. Fred completely subscribed to this view—but with a twist. For Fred, hard work was all about money. It was a recurring theme throughout his life. When he found his trade as a construction worker, he took pride in his accomplishments, as haphazard as many an extension or wall he built may have been. The bottom line with Fred was that there was always an angle, and his motivations were always multifaceted.

Moorcourt Cottage, where the West family lived, is located in the remote village of Much Marcle. So secluded was the village—and the West residence—that the Wests rarely mixed with outsiders, even other people from the village. For Walter West, this was a situation that suited him just fine, for he was almost certainly an incestuous pedophile. The dysfunctional world created within the confines of Moorcourt Cottage would leave an indelible print on the brain of Frederick West. The intense sexual flavor that permeated the home, courtesy of Fred's deviant father, would be a ripe breeding ground for one of the most fiendish sex killers that ever lived.

With such a terrible father, it is not unreasonable to think that young Freddy would have turned to his mother for support. But he found no real comfort there either, for it is highly likely that Frederick West was sexually abused by his mother from a very early age. There is even speculation that he lost his virginity to her. As he grew up, Fred became a classic mommy's boy and spent a lot of time in her company. The bond between mother and son was intense. When Fred's crimes were later revealed, Daisy, going well beyond even a normal mother's love, refused to accept that her boy could ever do any wrong.

Fred West practiced bestiality. This was a predilection that he did not develop in isolation. He later told of an occasion where his father revealed to him that if he were to slip a sheep's hind legs down the front of his Wellington boots while assaulting it, it could not run away. This is not the sort of father-son bonding that makes for happy, functional families, and Walter West's tips in bestiality formed only part of the code of conduct that he recommended to Fred. Walter West's view of life was that you should do whatever you want so long as it gives you pleasure. There were no boundaries. "Do whatever you want, just don't get caught doing it," he would instruct young Fred.

Fred grew into a full-fledged psychopath. When not working alongside his family in the fields around their home, he would often go off by himself, retreating into the countryside for hours at a time. He used these opportunities to experiment with his sexuality on animals, and indulged in increasingly violent sexual fantasies.

As he grew older, so his storytelling became more outrageous. People came to accept it as just Fred's way. He could not string a sentence together without lacing it with some kind of fabrication. Everyone took it in good humor and some of the local girls even found Fred's incessant line of patter quite charming. Suddenly, the prospect of forming sexual relationships with women began to open up to Fred. For a young man with confused and obsessive ideas regarding sex, this was a potentially dangerous development.

On the evening of November 28, 1958, Fred West crashed his prized 125cc James motorcycle into a car traveling the other direction. He had been riding at full speed and suffered several injuries, including a serious head wound. Being an outrageous embellisher of the truth, Fred later claimed that he had been pronounced dead after the crash and had only miraculously revived once he had been placed on the mortuary slab. What isn't in doubt is that he did lay unconscious in a ditch for some time until help arrived. The head trauma that West experienced in this accident was to have far-reaching consequences. It may well have served to exacerbate his already twisted way of thinking. In the words of Dr. David A. Holmes, the criminologist and forensic profiler:

> Like many unfortunate children, Fred did inherit brain abnormalities from his parents, who had problems themselves. This very much reached a crescendo after the accident, which not only caused great damage to his body, and the shortening of a leg, but delivered a massive amount of damage to his head and, therefore, to his brain... and the part of the brain that gets the head-on particular damage is the frontal cortex, the frontal lobe which contains the elements of what makes us a moral person that will give you a sense of revulsion if you commit a particularly horrific act. Now, for Fred, these were damaged, so for someone who was already a little psychopathic suddenly the brakes were taken off completely, and this made him into a complete danger to society.

As if one traumatic head injury were not enough, Fred suffered another one a little later on in life. He was being his usual smutty self, attempting to grope a girl on a fire escape, when she lashed out at him. He lost his balance and fell over the side of the staircase, landing head-first on the concrete below. One side effect of this type of brain injury can be a marked increase in sexual aggression and, in the wake of these two instances of head trauma, many would bear testament to a change in West's personality.

Fred's recovery from the road accident was slow and humiliating. His nose was broken and, because of the leg-shortening injury, he now suffered from a pronounced limp. He also experienced violent mood swings and he began to compensate for the loss of his good looks by taking a much more aggressive approach with the local girls. If he wanted sex, and the girls refused, he would effectively rape them. From then on, sex for Fred was also about control and domination. For him, it provided a kind of comfort, a chance to establish or reestablish his dominance over women. Later, for example, he would frequently beat his first wife while gripped by an uncontrollable rage. His violence would be swift and merciless when it erupted and could be caused by the most mundane oversights on her part, such as being late with the evening meal.

At nineteen, Fred West, under mounting local pressure, was forced to leave the family home at Moorcourt Cottage. It had become public knowledge that he had been having sex with a thirteen-year-old girl—and that she was pregnant. The pregnancy was terminated and Fred West found he had some explaining to do to the Social Services. However, the authorities were somewhat taken aback when, instead of the expected repentance or shame that they expected from the scruffy young man, he greeted them with genuine puzzlement. "Doesn't every-body do it?" he meekly asked.

Fred soon left the village and went to sea, working his way around the world on a succession of ships. He would later meet and marry a Coatbridge prostitute named Catherine "Rena" Costello and take on her daughter, Charmaine, as his own. He would abuse the pair of them thoroughly, eventually murdering them both. When Fred married Rena she was already five months pregnant with another man's child. She was a strong character, very much like his own mother, and she would often put him in his place. It was probably the first time any woman outside his family had ever done this.

Charmaine West was born in March 1963 and was soon followed by a little sister, Anne Marie. Childhood for the two girls was far from traditional. Rena and Fred had a very on-and-off life together. Rena would disappear for weeks or months at a time, so sometimes Fred was left alone with the children and sometimes they were placed in foster care. When Rena was not around, Fred found a succession of young women to help him raise the kids. It was an unconventional upbringing for Charmaine and Anne Marie.

In 1965, Fred and Rena's turbulent relationship finally reached breaking point. Fred's violence finally drove Rena away, and she fled to her native Scotland. Fred was happy to let her go but not the children. He had already recruit-ed sixteen-year-old Anne McFall to act as their nanny. Anna, as she was known, soon became pregnant with his child. Although she was the last of Fred's victims to be recovered, Anna was the first woman he killed, disappearing in July 1967. She had become a nuisance to West, so she was killed. It would be twenty-seven years before her body would be found buried in Letterbox Field near Much Marcle. The body had been decapitated and dismembered, and was found with the skeleton of her unborn child. Professor Bernard Knight recalls West's revelation of this particular slaying. "Fred said he buried her under a tree, but he didn't say which tree it was. He was a bit vague about all this, or so I was told. There was a gigantic hole in the ground for the second body. It looked like something from Tutankhamun's Tomb or something." Once Fred had murdered Anne McFall there was to be no going back.

Rosemary Pauline Letts was born on November 29, 1953. Given her own troubled upbringing it seems inevitable that she would one day find Fred West and become his wife and partner in crime. It was almost destiny.

Rosemary's parents, Daisy and Bill Letts, experienced between them a frightening range of mental health problems. Daisy suffered from disabling depression and, while carrying Rosemary, had undergone electro-convulsive shock therapy in an attempt to suppress her burgeoning depressive illness. Bill Letts had weighty cerebral problems, too. He was later diagnosed as a schizophrenic and was undoubtedly a longtime sufferer of paranoia. He was also an extremely obsessive-compulsive personality. He had served for a long time in the Navy and insisted that his home be run with the kind of ritual rigidity that he was used to on board ship. If the house was not kept spotless at all times he would hand out fearful beatings, to his wife especially.

As with Myra Hindley, until she moved in with Granny Maybury, little Rosemary had to endure the sometimes nightly spectacle of her psychotic father beating her mother with brutal abandon. To compensate, Rosie did all she could to please her father. The relationship between father and daughter would be a special one, intimate to the point of inappropriateness, until it became fully sexual. It was the sort of relationship only someone like Fred West would be able to understand.

Rosemary was such a docile child that her nickname was "Dozy Rosie." Of course, her relationship with her father must have contributed to this. She was most definitely daddy's girl. She knew what her father wanted from her, and she fully acquiesced. The sexual abuse that he subjected her to continued right up to—and after—the point at which she met Fred West.

When life in the Letts household in Bishop's Cleve, Gloucester, finally became too much for Daisy to bear, she gathered up her children and moved out—but she left Rose behind. It was almost as if Daisy accepted the unbreakable bond that existed between Bill and Rose and decided to leave them to their fate, salvaging the rest of the family instead.

But although it appeared as if Rose was being abandoned as a helpless victim, things were more complex than that. Despite being academically backward, Dozy Rosie was able to manipulate her father in ways nobody else could. She may have been slow at school but she was no dummy. Rose would become rapaciously sexual as a teenager and, at just fifteen, would move on to a relationship with Fred West, a man twelve years her senior. This caused her father much consternation and jealousy. It was almost as if the tables had been turned on Bill Letts.

Rose knew how to play men. She gave them whatever they wanted and in return they ultimately became dependent on her. Rose Letts, as she would later demonstrate at her infamous murder trial, had nerves of steel. Mentally, she never buckled.

When Fred West, the confident, cocky older man came on the scene he sized Rosemary up right away. She lit up like a neon sign to him and his natural-born predator's roving eye saw in the overtly sexual teenager his ideal mate. Rose in turn was quick to appraise Fred as another abuser. He was her father all over again, but there was something dark about him. He exuded a sense of danger and there was something crazy and exciting about him. He offered her a limitless world of sexual opportunity and she believed that he would introduce her to the greatest thrills imaginable. In a way, he did. In the words of Anthony Daniels, author of *So Little To Be Done... the testament of a serial killer*, "When Fred met Rose, he recognized what one might call a "soulmate," and that's why he was attracted to her. They had a kind of interlocking psychopathology background so that they played off each other, and their fantasies coincided, probably."

Once Fred had found his soulmate in Rose he now had the problem of what to do with Rena. Having tried and failed to mold Rena to his way of living, Fred decided that it was time for her to go. Rose was the sort of seemingly compliant sexual dynamo that he had always craved and the very existence of Rena now seemed to Fred to be a kind of living affront to his macho self-image. Fred and Rose moved into a cramped apartment at 25 Midland Road, Gloucester, which to Fred symbolized a fresh start. It was going to be a case of "out with the old and in with the new." Fred had already killed one woman, Anne McFall, so he knew that he was capable of doing it again. But before he killed Rena, Fred was to commit another shocking act of murder—against his step-daughter Charmaine.

In October 1970 Rose gave birth to her and Fred's first child, Heather Ann. Motherhood didn't come naturally to Rose. She was still young herself and, given her own upbringing, didn't understand what normal parenting was. "Breasts are for fucking, not breastfeeding," she once told her solicitor Leo Goatley. She also had a learning disability that meant she was childlike in many ways herself. Although it would be easy to think that this would make her more empathetic to children, the truth is that she was jealous of and confrontational with young children. She did not enjoy having her authority challenged by Heather. In many ways, she treated children more as dolls or toys than as human beings.

One consequence of Heather's birth was that now Fred and Rose had their own child. Charmaine, Rena's child who until now Fred had raised as his own, was now in some sense surplus to requirements. Sometime in June 1971, while Fred West was on parole and coming to the end of a nine-month prison sentence for theft, eight-year-old Charmaine disappeared. All evidence points to Rose being involved in Charmaine's death along with Fred. If this is the case, it meant that they were now in it together and that there was no going back. Fred and Rose's joint murder of Charmaine was an incredibly bonding experience. The emotional and psychological impact that such an act creates in its perpetrators is hard to fathom. The joint murder of a child creates a link between two people that can never be severed. The murder of Charmaine also set a precedent: If anyone ever threatened to come between Fred and Rose again they now knew how to deal with it.

Of course, now that Charmaine was gone there was one other person who could definitely come between Fred and Rose—Rena. When she came looking for her child, Fred took action. Rena was last seen alive in the autumn of 1971 and her remains were not discovered until more than twenty years later. By the beginning of 1972, with Charmaine and Rena out of his life forever, Fred took Rose to their new home at 25 Cromwell Street.

Cromwell Street was the perfect place for this dysfunctional couple to move to. As journalist Hugh Worsnip points out, "25 Cromwell Street would become the most infamous address in the world. It is inhabited by a moving population who were drifting around, or who had left home for some reason, or who couldn't easily be traced, and that is one of the reasons why Fred remained undetected for so many years." It was here, at 25 Cromwell Street, that Fred would create his private empire. This anonymous neighborhood provided the perfect cover for the Wests' lustful and homicidal nature.

One of the practical benefits of 25 Cromwell Street was that it was a house in need of repair. As a construction worker, Fred would work on the house himself. He put in a playroom for the children and extended the kitchen, taking an inordinate amount of pride in his home improvements. But it was the cellar to which Fred was obsessively drawn. It was to be his own private kingdom. He even joked to a neighbor that he intended to soundproof the cavernous room and convert it into a torture chamber.

Fred West wasted no time in introducing incest into his home. He had been raping his daughter Anne Marie regularly since she was eight years old. It is thought that he similarly abused his daughters with Rose, and Heather was murdered in part because of her intention to expose the secret torment she had endured from Fred.

The Wests used Cromwell Street to carry out their perverse sexual desires. Fred enjoyed prostituting his wife and had an obsession with the idea of a well-endowed Jamaican man taking Rose to bed while he listened in or spied on them. The couple amassed a huge collection of pornography. Later after his arrest, in two separate searches of 25 Cromwell Street, police uncovered literally hundreds of explicit sexual films and videos, both commercial and homemade. Fred boasted an impressive assortment of sex memorabilia, featuring not only films and magazines but dildos, leather and rubber outfits, masks, whips, a plethora of restraints and harnesses and torture devices. He especially enjoyed advertising Rose's services as a prostitute in contact magazines and reveled in filming many of her sexual encounters with paying customers. Many of the films had bondage and sado-masochistic themes. These featured spanking, domination, flagellation, torture (from nipple-clamping to electroshock) and, ultimately, snuff. Fred had even offered some of his home movies to a local video store proprietor as under-the-counter merchandise.

In November 1972, seventeen-year-old Caroline Owens was hitchhiking from Tewkesbury to her home in Cinderford. She had been on a regular visit to see her boyfriend, and was waiting on the street for a ride from a friend when a grey Ford car drew up and the couple inside offered her a ride. Caroline recalls, "[Rose] seemed pretty cheerful. She said, 'Where are you going to?' And I said, 'Cinderford' and she said, 'We're from Gloucester and we'll take you all the way back.' They started to tell me about their family and that they had three little girls and asked me if I would like to be their nanny. I was really excited because I had always dreamed of being a little girl's nanny. You know, everything seemed all right. It seemed very romantic and glamorous. I was going to escape from my home and go and live this fairytale." But Caroline's dream job would soon turn into a nightmare.

Caroline Owens had not been living at the Wests' for long when one day Fred casually revealed to her that Anne Marie had lost her virginity. Anne Marie was just eight years old. Caroline was shocked and confused. She quickly realized that Anne Marie was being beaten and sexually abused by her father. Once Fred had shared this shocking secret with Caroline, things rapidly spiraled out of control. Fred propositioned Caroline and explained to her that he and Rose were part of a sex circle with other men and asked if Caroline would like to join. Disgusted by these revelations, Caroline fled the house, vowing never to return.

A couple of months later, Caroline was standing in her usual hitchhiking spot close to her boyfriend's house when the Wests' car pulled up beside her. Her first instinct was to run away, but she didn't. Rose rolled down the window and apologized for her husband's poor behavior. She also told Caroline that the children were missing her and would she reconsider coming back. In a moment of weakness she would forever regret, Caroline climbed into the car and drove off with Fred and Rose. She recalls:

> Everything was fine. We went through Gloucester and the talk was about the children. As soon as we got into the country, Fred asked if I would like sex tonight. I said, "No. Don't start that kind of conversation up again." And he said, "Go on, Rose, have a feel and see if she's wet." With that she just pushed her hand down my crotch. We started fighting. About two miles out of Gloucester, Fred pulled up by the side of the road, turned around in his seat and punched me in the head until I was unconscious. When I came to, Fred had the door open. He had already tied my hands behind my back with my scarf, and was wrapping parcel tape all the way around my face as a gag, and took me back to Cromwell Street.

They eventually arrived at the house where, still bound and gagged, Caroline was taken into a bedroom and held captive for the next twelve hours. During this time she was beaten and subjected to what she called an "intimate medical examination of [my] body and genitalia" by Fred and Rose. At one point, Fred removed his belt, and buckle end first, slapped it hard between Caroline's legs. Then, as Rose performed her own indecent assault on the terrified young woman, Fred had sex with Rose from behind. In genuine fear for her life, Caroline was eventually left alone with Fred. "I thought he was going to take me down to the cellar but he obviously had second thoughts and he raped me. Then he started crying and told me that if I promised I wouldn't tell anyone he'd touched me, and I'd come back to live with them, he'd let me go," she says. Fearful that she would be killed if she didn't agree with West, Caroline agreed to stay quiet. She promised to return to 25 Cromwell Street and resume her post as the childrens' nanny. However, as soon as she left the house she went straight to the police.

Fred and Rose pled guilty to the kidnapping and sexual assault of Caroline, and were put on trial. But by the time the case came to court Caroline had decided that she was too frightened to give evidence. Incredibly, Fred and Rose West were fined just $50 each. No custodial sentences were handed down and the deranged couple were free to pick up where they had left off.

The $50 fines sent the Wests a very clear message that, even if you do slip up, you can still get away with even the most horrific crimes. They also learned that, all in all, it was best not to get caught and that taking extreme steps to ensure this would mean that they could go unpunished. Having learned this valuable lesson, they would choose their victims with care from then on. They realized that there were plenty of people around who would not be missed. To find them, they used exactly the same techniques that some religious groups use—seek out the weak and vulnerable and offer them protection, hope and a sense of belonging. Fred and Rose's appetites for sexual violence and death had been whetted and they wanted more. They'd made mistakes in the past and had been lucky to get away with it. They would plan things more carefully in the future. There was no way they would let their future victims escape and go running to the police the way that Caroline had.

Fred and Rose became adept at spotting the types of girls that can be classed as "less than dead," that is, a person who could be safely kidnapped and murdered without being missed: prostitutes, runaways and girls who have become estranged from their families and friends.

Once Fred and Rose had selected their prey, the girls were taken back to Cromwell Street and, ultimately, down into the cellar. The full record of events that took place in that cellar will never be known, but from the few testimonies that we have we can make some accurate speculations. For example, it is absolutely certain that the cellar was routinely used as a place of sexual torture and abuse. Victims were hung up, bound, stripped and gagged for long periods of time, enduring extreme pain. It should be remembered that Fred had very little idea of how to exercise restraint when it came to inflicting suffering on others. To force others to undergo intolerable, almost continuous and protracted pain and injury would incite in him just a fraction, if any, of the revulsion a normal person would experience in this situation. According to Dr. David A. Holmes, "He would not have had the same sense of revulsion that most would have of stripping the body, and deciding how to dispose of it. He would be industrious about this, and this would have set him apart from many attempted killers and serial killers in that he was very energetic about the way he went about things."

Fred West fitted a beam across the cellar and screwed hooks into it. He later revealed how he hung girls from the beam for days at a time, and how some of the corpes that he left there began to mummify. Ultimately, the girls' bodies were dismembered and their remains were buried beneath the cellar floor. Over time, Fred and Rose became skilled at taking bodies apart. According to Professor Bernard Knight, "The bodies had been dismembered. All the heads had been taken off, and there were small cuts on the vertebrae, usually in the same place on the necks. All the legs had been taken off at the hip, and there were little cut marks around the head of the thigh bones—they were pretty well done, I think." When there was literally no more room in the cellar for any more bodies, Fred concreted over the floor and converted the room into a bedroom for his children.

Fred and Rose had now perfected their *modus operandi* and over the next fourteen years would kidnap, torture and murder almost at will. But each successive murder would require them to push the boundaries of sado-sexual behavior further and further. Each had their role to fulfill, and both Fred and Rose played out these roles with an ever-increasing level of depravity. Rose's role was as the abusive one, but also the one who was in control of the situation. Fred's role was to push back the boundaries of sadism and bondage. Together they made a terrifying team, urging each other on from one excess to the other. When they wanted their victims to scream more they knew just where to cut that little bit deeper; they knew what torture caused the most pain and how to regulate it. With their victims bound, gagged and masked they could play out any scenario their twisted imaginations could conjure up.

Fred and Rose sunk to such depths that it was entirely probable that one of them could easily have ended up as the other's next victim. Given Fred's track record, the victim was more likely to be Rose. Of course, Rose knew how to handle a man and she knew how to give Fred what he wanted, but underlying their relationship was the idea that what stopped them from turning on each other was that there was still an endless stream of young girls to take out their murderous impulses on. Their killing may even have been competitive, driven by a need to show each other that they still had "what it takes" and that each was not ready to be the other's victim just yet.

By June 1987 the West's oldest daughter, Heather, was sixteen. She had suffered both physical and sexual abuse at the hands of her parents all of her life. Until then she had always been their silent victim, but she was threatening to become a problem. Fred and Rose began to sense that Heather was about to talk to someone about her abuse and so it was decided that she should be stopped. Heather was murdered one day when the other children had gone off to school and Fred buried her under what subsequently became the patio. In Fred's mind, he was merely disposing of something he had no further use for. In the opinion of Dr. David Holmes, "If Heather had been able to survive and continue, she may have brought the whole façade down and that could not be allowed. To some degree, they committed a very risky murder to show that they were in control to the rest of their children, and this murder probably led to their undoing."

Although Heather lay undiscovered beneath the patio at Cromwell Street for another eight years, her death was the first sign that Fred and Rose were becoming complacent. Instead of never referring to Heather again, they made a sick joke of her disappearance to their other children. Behave yourselves, they would say, or you will end up under the patio like Heather. In time, persistent rumors about Heather's disappearance soon reached the ears of a local policewoman, Detective Savage. Disturbed by what she heard, Savage convinced her superiors that it was worth following up and arranged for a warrant to dig up the West's patio. It was the beginning of the end of Fred and Rose's killing spree.

What direct evidence is there that Rosemary West was involved in all these murders? Fred West was a rapist and killer before he met her, and continued to be one during their marriage. The Jury that convicted Rose West on ten counts of murder in October 1995 had to rely heavily on circumstantial findings. It is also a fact that, had Fred West not hanged himself on New Years Day 1995, he would have stood trial for murders that Rosemary, until that time, had not been charged with. After he committed suicide, many of these charges were pressed against Rose instead. The simple truth is that we may never know the full truth of Rose's role in these awful slayings because she has never once admitted culpability for any of them. It was assumed at trial that because she had participated in the sadistic sexual assault of Caroline Owens, she was a vicious abuser of her own children. Because she had lived for twenty years with a diseased psychopath, it was said, she must have known what he was doing in their basement. Compelling arguments indeed, but speculation nonetheless.

Theories regarding what really went on abound. For example, there is also speculation that the girls were not murdered in the house but were executed elsewhere and merely brought back to Cromwell Street for interment, or that West murdered "to order" for a local satanic cult. It is also said that there is a farmhouse where up to twenty-five of Fred's other victims lay dead and buried. Again, these are assertions with no evidential basis. Where Fred and Rose West are concerned, truth is never far from fiction.

Based on what we do know about serial killers, we can say that the majority of them have suffered from some form of child abuse. This is the case with both Fred and Rose West. Others, including Kenneth Bianchi, Michael Ross, John Wayne Gacy and Henry Lee Lucas, suffered head trauma during their formative years, as did Fred West.

As West grew up, his fantasies became more complex and sadistic. He was obsessed with bondage and deviant behaviour. Nothing aroused the man more than having a completely immobilized victim before him and at his complete mercy. West would torture and abuse them for hours on end. He would positively revel in his victims' terror, becoming enormously gratified by their pain and suffering. The bondage he placed them in became more refined and elaborate over time. The tortures became more ferocious, his sexual assaults more barbaric, as his craving grew uncontrollable and he sought bigger kicks. He delighted in mutilating victims while they squirmed in agony in their bonds. The more he killed, the more horrific the torment he dealt out. His antisocial sexual conduct can easily be traced along a continuum from mild abuse to mayhem.

Fred West began as a rapist. Notwithstanding Dr. Shipman, who killed a greater number of people, West ended his criminal career as Britain's most infamous sado-sexual serial killer. He graduated from the act of forced sex, to causing massive injury with any number of weapons: hammers, knives and tools from his beloved work box. West almost certainly indulged in sadistic torture, necrophilia and bizarre sexual experiments on his live victims. Once dead, they would be systematically taken to pieces—decapitated, dismembered and destroyed. A methodical and willful destruction of everything that had once made the victim human. A number of fingers, toes and wrist bones—even a shoulder blade and some kneecaps—were missing from the skeletal remains unearthed from a number of burial sites. All were removed and hidden somewhere by Fred, for his own reasons. There is also some evidence to suggest that cannibalism was among his many other sins.

There is little doubt that Fred West murdered many other women. One of whom is most certainly the missing fifteen-year-old waitress from Gloucester, Mary Bastholm, who vanished from a bus stop on January 6, 1968, just as Lucy Partington would five years later. In the final months of his life, West confessed to his son

Stephen that there was an old farm in the Gloucester area where "twenty or more" women lay buried. West had also lived in Glasgow in the 1960s, where he met his first wife Rena. During his time there, four young girls disappeared that all matched West's preferred victim criteria. At this time West had rented a garden allotment but rarely used the plot and eventually abandoned it. Police were unable to investigate the site because by the time West's crimes had come to light, the plot had been buried beneath Junction 22 of the M8 highway.

It does not take an investigative genius to work out that West was a sexual serial killer who felt the need to commit murder on a regular basis. It is unlikely that he resisted these urges for long, even if the bodies have not been found to back up this assertion. Serial killers are perfect killing machines. They are one-strike weapons that zero in on their targets and cause terrible destruction. By this criteria, it is our opinion that Frederick West was one of the most vicious and prolific serial killers in criminal history. With over thirty years of murder to his discredit and undoubtedly many additional bodies still as of now undiscovered, the man can only be described as a human monster.

When Fred West chose to hang himself in his prison cell at Winson Green, he had reached the end of a long line of mayhem. Facing the remainder of his worthless life behind bars and no longer able to rape, mutilate and kill with his usual frenzied gusto, there was no point for him to continue his life. Abandoning his previous allegiance to his wife, he took the quick way out. It was his last and ultimate act of control.

FBI HIGH RISK REGISTER—FRED WEST:

1. Alcohol abuse
2. Drug abuse
3. Psychiatric history
4. Criminal history
5. Sexual problems
6. Physical abuse
7. Psychological abuse
8/9. Dominant father figure aligned with a negative relationship with male caretaker figures
10. Negative relationships with both natural mother and or adoptive mother
11. Treated unfairly
12. Head trauma
13. Demon seed

1	2	3	4	5	6	7	8/9	10	11	12	13	%
0	0	X	X	X	X	X	XX	X	X	X	X	82.5

CHAPTER 4

JEFFREY DAHMER

"During dismemberment I saved the heart... also meat from the thigh, bicep, liver... cut it into small pieces, washed them off, put [them in] clear plastic freezer bags and put them on the floor of the freezer. Just as an escalation of trying something new... to satisfy. And I would cook it and then look at the picture and masturbate afterwards... it made me feel like they were part of me."

Dahmer in an interview with
Colonel Robert Ressler of the FBI

ON MONDAY, JULY 22, 1991, Jeffrey Dahmer was arrested and he confessed to having killed and dismembered seventeen young men. Parts of many of them were found in his apartment and removed by police in plastic bags.

The word spread rapidly, and journalists and TV crews were soon camped outside Dahmer's residence, informing the world that the Oxford Apartments on 924 N. 25th Street, Milwaukee, was the scene of a horrific series of homosexual serial murders. A decade earlier, the neighboring city of Chicago had seen a similar spell of murders in which a building contractor named John Wayne Gacy had killed thirty-three boys and hidden the bodies in the crawlspace under his house, beneath the garage floor or had thrown them in the slow-moving Des Plaines River.

In 1980, another homosexually motivated killer terrorized Los Angeles. William Bonin, the "Freeway Killer," had murdered up to forty-one boys in that city, while in 1973 Dean Corll took the lives of twenty-seven young men in Houston, Texas. The list goes on—in 1983, Randy Kraft was charged with sixty-seven young male homicides in California and Larry Eyler, operating across Chicago and Indiana killed twenty-three youths. So while Dahmer's crimes were not the first of their kind, nor the most extensive, there was something about the nature of Dahmer's murders that cemented them in the public's consciousness.

Born at 4:34 p.m. on Saturday, May 21, 1960, at the Evangelical Deaconess Hospital in Milwaukee, Jeffrey was the first child of Lionel and Joyce Dahmer. By all accounts he was the perfect baby, weighing 7 pounds and measuring 18 inches long, with auburn hair and luminously blue eyes. His only flaw was that he required casts on his legs for four months and had to wear lifts on his shoes until he was six years old.

Lionel was an engineering student at Milwaukee's Marquette University, and the couple lived with his mother

Catherine, a schoolteacher, in West Allis. In 1962 Lionel Dahmer obtained a degree in electrical engineering, and four years later he received a doctorate in analytical chemistry. Lionel was a hard worker, an achiever, who had little time to pay attention to his son. Jeffrey was later to describe him—with a touch of bitterness—as a "highly controlling and a strong character." Lionel's wife, Joyce, was equally controlling and strong. She was also neurotic, and as the years went by their marriage became increasingly stormy. Jeffrey became accustomed to the sight and sound of his parents quarreling. On at least one occasion, their fighting resulted in a physical assault on each other.

Towards the end of 1963 Jeffrey was treated for an ear infection and mild pneumonia, and his parents were told that they would have to watch out for a growing hernia condition. Surgery was eventually performed on March 19, 1964, and when Jeffrey recovered he found himself in agonizing pain. He also suffered the first trauma of his life—he thought for a time that his genitals had been cut off. Three changes of school and home in two years did nothing for his sense of security, since his father's work took him to Ames, Ohio, then to Doylestown in October 1966 before they rented a house in Barberton.

At Doylestown, the arguments between Joyce and her husband increased along with her hypersensitivity and depression. She made a fuss of trivial matters and initiated arguments in order to enjoy the pleasure of reconciliation with Lionel. A hypochondriac, she began to take pills to calm her nerves, doubling the dosage when they failed to have the desired effect. There are also suggestions that she tried to kill herself with an overdose of Seconal, though it may be the case that she simply took too many pills out of carelessness. Either way, it indicates the behavior of a troubled and desperate woman. And all of this negativity was mirrored onto six-year-old Jeffrey.

When his mother became pregnant with another child and was sick for six months, Jeffrey began to feel neglected. His brother David was born on December 18, 1966, and Jeffrey felt more abandoned and left out than ever before.

Just as their stay at Doylestown was short-lived, so was their sojourn at Barberton. Evenually, the Dahmers found a permanent base at 4480 West Bath Road in Bath, Ohio, in 1968. It was their third move in two years and their sixth address since marriage.

The year they moved into their new home—according to Lionel Dahmer—Jeffrey was sexually assaulted in the nearby woods. Lionel Dahmer believes this event marked the beginning of his son's sexual problems.

Jeffrey was a quiet and gentle boy, and like so many youths who later in life become serial killers, he was known as a melancholy loner and would spend much of his time wandering and fantasizing in the woods. There was a solitary game he would play which he called "Infinity Land." It was quite a complicated game for one so young, and although it indicated above average intelligence, the concept was vaguely sinister. It was comprised of sticks that represented men and involved them disappearing one by one into a vortex—a somewhat bleak pursuit and a hallmark of an obviously lonely person. But Jeffrey also liked attention and gained it from his school friends by clowning around, making faces and flapping his arms like a comic Frankenstein's monster. His sense of humor was grotesque and sometimes cruel. Oddly enough, although he had a high IQ, Jeffrey's school grades were usually low—a sure sign of emotional disturbance and an inability to concentrate. At this very young age Jeffrey Dahmer was already living in a world of his own.

The Dahmers usually sat down for dinner together and at ten years old, Jeffrey turned to his father one evening and asked him what would happen if the chicken bones left on the plate were to be dropped in bleach. Lionel already knew of his son's interest in dissection, and thinking that this was a commendable scientific curiosity, it made him happy to see Jeffrey show such initiative. Lionel prepared a pot and dropped the bones into the bleach while his son waited patiently and unblinking for the result. As Jeffrey progressed through childhood, he became more and more fascinated with dead animals. He would collect road kill from along the highway and take these creatures home to experiment on, enthralled by their passivity. The sight and touch of glistening viscera was a source of arousal for the disturbed youngster. As he learned to masturbate it was to thoughts of fetal pig dissections and mutilated animal remains that he would return to again and again. When Jeffrey discovered that he was homosexual, images of naked men fused in his mind with these disturbing images of death and destruction.

It was to be a life-long, inextricable union and Jeffrey soon developed more intricate fantasies, one of which involved the abduction and subsequent intimate contact with a male jogger, whose route took him past the

Dahmer home at 4480 West Bath Road. Because he knew that the man would reject his advances, Jeffrey imagined striking the man with a baseball bat and then fondling and kissing him. One day, he took a baseball bat and waited at the side of the road. Providence, however, worked in the jogger's favor because on that particular day he did not come by and a troubled Jeffrey returned home with his bat, fantasies unfulfilled.

While Dahmer began to have fantasies about killing men and having sex with their corpses as early as age fourteen, he didn't do anything about it until just after he graduated from high school in June 1978, when he picked up a hitchhiker named Steven Hicks. They had sex and drank beer, but eventually Hicks wanted to leave. Dahmer couldn't stand the idea of Hicks deserting him, so he struck Hicks in the head with an 8-inch barbell. After a brief scuffle, Dahmer slammed down the weapon onto his victim's head a second time and Hicks fell unconscious. With the body at his mercy, Dahmer strangled Hicks until he was sure he was dead.

With the corpse now lying in front of him, Dahmer carefully removed Steven's clothing to reveal the beauty that had disturbed him. He ran his hands over the chest, caressed it and kissed it, then lay down beside the body. Finally, he stood above Steven's body and masturbated onto it. Realizing that he needed to get rid of the corpse as soon as possible, Dahmer dragged it down into the crawlspace of the family home, where he cut it into pieces and packaged up the severed parts in triple-lined plastic garbage bags. Hicks' I.D. and clothing were burned in the trash barrel about 160 feet from the house, and the following night he dumped the bags into a ravine 4 miles away. Ironically, Dahmer was stopped by the police as he drove out to the ravine that next evening, but was only briefly questioned and released without his car being searched. The life of Jeffrey Dahmer, and that of his victims, turned on that simple incident.

At the same time as that of his first murder, Jeffrey's parents were coming to the end of a long and messy divorce process. Because he was never close to his parents in the first place, their divorce meant they were even more emotionally unavailable to him at this time than ever before. He had nowhere to turn to satisfy his emotional needs or express unhappiness. It may even have been the case that Dahmer was in a sense autistic, incapable of feeling any real connection with his fellow human beings.

Jeffrey's first murder and the breakup of his family occurred when Dahmer was eighteen. He had just enrolled at Ohio State University, hoping to major in business studies, but clearly this was a troubled time in his life. As his studies got underway Jeffrey developed a severe drinking problem that destroyed his will to work. His father visited him one day and found his son's room full of empty liquor bottles. Dahmer even resorted to selling his blood at a local blood bank in order to get the money to buy alcohol. He would also take alcohol into class and get drunk while his peers studiously took notes. When $120, a watch and a radio went missing from his dorm, Dahmer was questioned by police, but no charge was made. One fellow student later saw Jeffrey lying drunk on Columbus street. It looked as though nothing could save Jeffrey from self-destruction.

Dahmer lasted only one semester before leaving the university. Seeing no other career opportunities, Dahmer joined the army and signed on for three years. In 1979, he was posted to Baumholder in West Germany as a medic. However, he continued to drink heavily and spent much of his free time listening to rock and heavy metal music on a Walkman, totally withdrawn from the world. Jeffrey's fellow soldiers felt that he was going downhill. Eventually, alcohol rendered him so inefficient that he was discharged with nine months still left to serve. As he left, Dahmer told his colleagues, "Some day you'll hear of me again."

Apparently, Dahmer didn't kill anyone while he was in the army, a fact that was later corroborated by an exhaustive investigation by the German police. After his discharge Jeffrey went to live in Florida, before returning to Ohio. Once back home, he dug up Hick's body, pounded the decomposing corpse with a sledgehammer and scattered the remains in the woods.

In October 1981, twenty-one-year-old Dahmer was arrested for drunkenness. His father decided that his son would do better if he moved in with his grandmother in West Allis, Wisconsin. Things seemed to calm down for a while, until Jeffrey got drunk one evening and dropped his pants in the company of a group of people. This bizarre exhibitionistic display was one of several he engaged in around this time, but he did however manage to remain out of trouble for a further four years until September 1986—when he was arrested for masturbating in front of two boys. Jeffrey was placed on parole for a year.

During this time when he was living in West Allis with his grandmother, Jeffrey's urge to kill became prevalent again. Dahmer wanted to repeat the act he had committed on Hicks but was also actively wrestling with his inner demons that thirsted for blood. Unlike so many serial killers, Dahmer was able to resist his deadly compulsion—as far as we know—for a number of years. But as 1987 came around, he knew he was fighting a losing battle. In desperation, he read the Bible for solace. He also stole a male mannequin from a department store in the vain hope that by sexually interacting with the inanimate male symbol, he would have no need to go out and risk offending again. It didn't work.

Dahmer soon found himself visiting gay bathhouses, where he first began to experiment with drugging his partners. Crushed sedatives normally did the trick and he quickly acquired a dubious reputation around these and other known homosexual haunts. The word was out. "Stay away from him," people were warned, there was something definitely very wrong about a guy who went around drugging people all the time. District Attorney Michael McCann describes Dahmer's technique at this time: "Some of the men he victimized were homosexual, some were not. He would approach them and suggest that he would like to take pictures of them, would they come to his apartment where he had already prepared a drug which he would induce them to drink." Colonel Robert Ressler of the FBI comments, "[Dahmer] said once he had snapped the lock on the door and the person was in his apartment, he'd become more aggressive, more powerful. It was almost like a psychological transformation. He would become more sexually aroused." From simply taking his victims home and drugging them, it was just a short step for Dahmer to move on to murder.

The balmy evening of Sunday, July 22, 1992 would be one well-remembered by the citizens of Milwaukee. Events began to unfold when police officers Robert Rauth and Rolf Mueller were flagged down at an intersection on North 25th Street by a distressed young man with a handcuff dangling from his wrist. The thirty-two-year-old black male identified himself as Tracy Edwards and hysterically blurted out that he had been the victim of a deranged attack perpetrated by a "freak."

Earlier that evening, Edwards had been drinking with his attacker at his apartment, when his host had suddenly brandished a large knife and slapped a handcuff on his wrist. He had tried to handcuff Edwards completely but Edwards had remained as calm as he could and reasoned with the man that he didn't need to be restrained. Edwards saw that his attacker did not want him to leave, so Edwards reassured the man that he had no intention of going anywhere.

The man forced Edwards to accompany him to his bedroom. Together they watched the movie *Exorcist III* while Edwards' captor, seated alongside him on the bed and armed with a large knife, swayed back and forth as if in a trance and chanted some lunatic mantra. As Edwards stared at the TV screen, terrified but trying to remain cool, the man casually informed him that he would like to eat his heart. Realizing he must escape at the first chance, Edwards bided his time until he saw an opportunity. While the "freak" sat lost in his own demented trance, Edwards struck him a blow to the face and ran for the door. The guy almost grabbed Edwards as he opened the door to the apartment and ran down the corridor.

Upon hearing this story the incredulous officers decided to investigate further. Accompanying Edwards back to Dahmer's block, they were led up several flights of stairs to apartment No. 213, the scene of the alleged assault. A brisk rap on the door summoned the occupant, who identified himself as Jeffrey Lionel Dahmer, age thirty-one. Immediately, a sickly stench hit the two cops and, in the yellowy light, the man's skin was so pale it seemed as though it rarely saw sunlight. Dahmer, showing no outward visible sign of emotion, allowed the officers entry to his apartment.

Dahmer was at first cooperative, if a little docile in his demeanor. When the officers asked for the keys to Edwards' handcuffs Dahmer pointed toward his bedroom. However, he told them that he didn't know exactly where the key was and that the only way to remove the cuffs was to saw off Edwards' hand. Perturbed, the officers began to move towards Dahmer's bedroom, at which point he became animated for the first time and leaped into the path of Officer Mueller, who ordered him to back off.

In Dahmer's bedroom, Mueller immediately spotted the knife Edwards had said Dahmer threatened him with. He also noticed a half-open top drawer of a dresser. Inside were dozens of Polaroid photographs depicting nude men. On closer inspection, Mueller quickly recoiled—some of the images showed decapitated and dismembered human bodies. Judging by the décor, the pictures had been taken in this very apartment. In the words of District Attorney Michael McCann, "One of the officers saw some pictures of the skinning of a human being... he looked at the pictures, and was surprised that he was in the very room where those pictures had been taken. He yelled out to his partner, 'Grab him!'" Dahmer tried to leap up but was quickly restrained by Rauth.

Mueller approached the refrigerator, which Dahmer had previously told Edwards not to open when he went for a beer. Inside Mueller found a human head laying face down in a box. Mueller recoiled in horror and slammed the door shut. "For what I did, I should be dead," mumbled Dahmer, now restrained on the floor.

Police would eventually recover a frightening assortment of remains from this human slaughterhouse. There was a collection of skulls, for example, some bleached and others hand- or spray-painted. Three additional severed heads were found in one upright freezer compartment, and locked in ice at the base of the unit was a bag loaded with flesh and internal organs. Another freezer held two hearts, each individually wrapped in plastic bags. A thick slab of muscle tissue was also recovered.

On the floor of a cupboard lay a large kettle containing a pair of human hands and an excised set of genitals. In the bottom drawer of a metal filing cabinet in Dahmer's bedroom police found a complete human skeleton, along with the dried remnants of somebody's scalp and another penis, shriveled with age. A fifty-seven-gallon blue plastic drum sat in the corner of the bedroom. Back at the crime lab this sealed receptacle was found to hold three human torsos marinating in their own juices.

As this grim work of retrieval went on, Dahmer calmly gave a horrendous and detailed recital of what he had been up to for the last several years. When he was finished, he had accounted for the murders of sixteen men. He would later reveal that he had committed another homicide many years earlier, when he was just seventeen.

In addition to listing his murders, Dahmer went into gruesome details regarding what he did to the bodies. In the words of Detective Patrick Kennedy, "What he did was he bought an adaptable grill, which he put on his gas stove. We found this. He said he would sear [the meat of his victims] on both sides. He added some condiments to it... some vegetables, mushrooms and onions... and during the month before we caught him, this was pretty much the only meat he ate." Along with grotesque revelations of tenderizing a man's bicep and applying steak sauce before consuming it, ejaculating into torn open ribcages, draping himself with bloody entrails, and the fact that it takes about an hour to boil a human head, Jeffrey Dahmer explained that he had struggled for a number of years to deny his murderous impulses.

He revealed that following his first murder at seventeen years old, he did not kill again for nine years. His resolve finally snapped during a drunken sexual liaison one night at the Ambassador Hotel in September 1987. He told officers that he had blacked out and that when he came to there was a dead man in the room with him. His victim, twenty-four-year-old Steven Tuomi, had blood pouring from his mouth and his chest had been crushed where Dahmer, immersed in some powerful yet unremembered rage, had beaten him with his fists. Detective

Kennedy explains Dahmer's methodology: "Dahmer lay with the men, listening to their hearts. He trained himself to know when they were coming out of the drug-induced coma by their breathing because it would start to get sharp and short from the long, slow drug-induced sleep... and that's when he knew it was time to kill them."

The murders followed thick and fast after this break in his homicidal resolve. Whether he picked men up in gay bars, nightclubs, shopping malls or bus stops, Dahmer would normally lure them to his home on the pretext of wanting to photograph them for cash, or spend time watching movies and having a drink with them, for which he said he would pay them.

As each victim was lured to his apartment, Dahmer's treatment of them became ever more depraved. In the words of Detective Kennedy, "His crimes grew on, and the momentum grew stronger... as did his want to look for this perfect orgasm, to do more and more things in order to have this satisfying orgasm. It started with having pornographic homosexual sex, and then having homosexual sex with the people in the baths, having sex and killing, and then having sex with dead people, and then having sex with the viscera, and then eating the people he had sex with to get this superb orgasmic experience."

Fifteen more young men, mostly black and Hispanic, would die by Dahmer's hands. One victim was a fourteen-year-old Laotian boy named Konerak Sinthasomphone who, in a cruel twist of fate, had a brother who years before had been indecently assaulted by Dahmer. In this tragic case, police officers had returned the naked youth, who had managed to escape from Dahmer's apartment, straight back to the killer's lair. It was their reasoning that Konerak was a homosexual who was drunk or high on drugs. Closer inspection would have revealed that the boy had had a hole drilled in his head. Dahmer, playing the concerned older "boyfriend" for the cops, was allowed to take charge of the young man. Take charge he certainly did, by strangling Sinthasomphone to death the moment the officers had left.

Dahmer explained to Detective Patrick Kennedy how he had cut the throat of one victim, but had found this method of slaughter not only very messy but it also caused "too much pain" to the dying man. Subsequent victims were therefore drugged and strangled. For Dahmer, it was not so much the act of murder itself that excited him but the aftermath of his actions. One person who understands Dahmer's psychology like few others is Nico Claux, the so-called "Vampire of Paris," a convicted cannibal who first tasted human flesh while working in a Paris mortuary. He explains, "There is a state of euphoria right after you have [eaten human flesh for the first time]... a high. You are like the top of the mountain. [Dahmer] was not interested in having a relationship with a willing victim... he wanted total control over the human body to do whatever he wanted." Claux continues, "So, I can really, really relate to somebody like [Dahmer]. I can understand what went through his mind and what his obsessions were. He was really concerned with the aesthetics... like how beautiful they looked in his eyes... his victims he would pose in twisted positions."

JEFFREY DAHMER'S VICTIMS

Steven Hicks, age nineteen. Murdered: June 1978

Steven Tuomi, age twenty-four. Murdered:
September 15, 1987

James Doxtator, age fourteen. Murdered:
January 16, 1988

Richard Guerrero, age twenty-three. Murdered:
March 24, 1988

Anthony Sears, age twenty-six. Murdered:
March 25, 1989

Raymond Smith, age thirty-two. Murdered:
May 20, 1990

Eddie Smith, age twenty-seven. Murdered:
June 24, 1990

Ernest Miller, age twenty-three. Murdered:
September 2, 1990

David Thomas, age twenty-three. Murdered:
September 24, 1990

Curtis Straughter, age nineteen. Murdered:
February 17, 1991

Errol Lindsey, age nineteen. Murdered:
April 7, 1991

Tony Hughes, age thirty-one. Murdered:
May 24, 1991

Konerak Sinthasomphone, age fourteen. Murdered:
May 27, 1991

Matt Turner, age twenty. Murdered: June 30, 1991

Jeremiah Weinberg, age twenty-three. Murdered:
July 15, 1991

Oliver Lacy, age twenty-three. Murdered:
July 15, 1991

Joseph Bradehoft, age twenty-five. Murdered:
July 19, 1991

This catalogue of horror would later be recycled in sickening detail at Dahmer's televised trial. His defense was
that he was insane. The prosecution argued otherwise. A
jury ultimately declared him mentally competent and
thus found him guilty of the fifteen murders he was ultimately tried for. He received sentences totaling more
than nine hundred years. In the end, he served just a mere
fraction of his sentence. On November 28, 1994, Jeffrey
Dahmer was clubbed to death with a broom handle by fellow inmate and convicted murderer Christopher Scarver
in the Columbia Correctional Facility at Portage.

Among the many controversies surrounding the murders committed by Jeffrey Dahmer is the one regarding
the ethnicity of his victims. Given that most of those
murdered were of African–American or Hispanic origin,
it has inevitably been asked whether Dahmer's murders
were fueled by racial hatred. Jeffrey Dahmer always
denied this, stating instead that he simply found these
men more attractive and that they tended to possess the
kind of hairless torsos he liked.

Dahmer was not a sexual sadist, at least not in the conventional sense. When he was arrested he was instantly
very candid with investigators, and the first thing he did
when he arrived at the police station was give a full confession. He claimed that his desire was never to cause his
victims suffering and that he only committed his atrocities upon them after death. He was adamant—he had never
wanted to cause them pain. One must, however, consider

this along with the fact that he has admitted to drilling holes in the heads of a number of living victims and pouring boiling water and acid into their craniums.

Dahmer's utterly irrational design in doing this was to create mindless automatons totally devoted to serving their master's sexual requirements. In the words of Colonel Robert Ressler, "He began fantasizing that he could make things much better for himself by creating a sex zombie, and the sex zombie would stay with him all the time and he would not have to murder anymore."

Dahmer himself admitted as much in an interview with Ressler, "I wasn't getting the satisfaction from having to kill people, so I took it to a new level. I had a hand drill that I used for home things like installing the security system...it drills a small bore hole in the skull... very quickly. And with a large syringe, I filled that up with acid, injected it into the frontal lobes of the victim to produce a zombie-like state."

Dahmer also had an unusual fetish for abdomens. This was in fact the most erotic part of the male form for him. We have seen photographs taken by the killer himself in which he has shattered and pried open a victim's chest cavity and removed various internal organs. The systematic destruction and the total dehumanization of a human body was a passion Dahmer shared with Fred West. To these men, the bodies became objects to be played with, items to be cut to pieces and posed in various positions for a demon and his camera.

Dahmer's distinct "signature" involved drugging a man senseless, engaging in what he called "light sex"—general fondling, fellating and masturbating his sleeping partner—before strangling him to death, then decapitating and dismembering the body and interacting sexually with the severed parts. He would retain mementos such as photographs, and even body parts.

Jeffrey Dahmer's killing spree is among the more gruesome in the annals of serial homicide. The sheer monstrousness of many of the acts he practiced on his victims is enough to question the man's sanity. However, he was found by the jury to be sane and we agree with this. Jeffrey Dahmer was clearly a sexual deviant of the highest magnitude and he was a man who had no regard for the people he slaughtered. He practiced the most abominable perversions on the dead, but he knew what he was doing and he knew that it was unacceptable to society at large. He knew he faced life imprisonment if apprehended. He took steps to conceal his crimes, and he only killed when it was safe for him to do so.

The truly horrific nature of his crimes can be attributed to an escalation of fantasies the man had nurtured since childhood. The more he killed, the more he experimented with his victims. In order to achieve the level of excitement he craved, Dahmer had to perpetrate more bizarre and ghastly acts upon his victims. As he matured as a killer, his appalling activities mushroomed. Towards the end he built a "shrine," using a black table and a number of the skulls and skeletons of his victims. He would adorn the altar with statues and sit himself at his creation, where he believed he would receive enormous rushes of power. He felt he would become as mighty as the psychotic heroes that appeared in his favorite horror movies. He even bought a pair of yellow contact lenses so that his eyes might resemble those of the malevolent Emperor figure from the *Star Wars* films. He also identified with the possessed man in *Exorcist I* and the deformed sadist, "Pinhead," from the *Hellraiser* movies. These characters are all-powerful, exceedingly potent figures. All are utterly evil, just as Dahmer had grown to view himself.

In the end, he was truly a lost soul. Consumed by his own nightmarish existence, this once-organized offender grew careless and haphazard. It was only a matter of time before the police caught up with him.

Several authorities on this case suggest that if Jeffrey had not turned to alcohol he may have become an "achiever," like his father. But we suggest that Jeffrey's formative years and his early behavior before he took to drinking indicate otherwise. In his late teens he was still a dropout, a nobody working in a chocolate factory. He had by this time been virtually alone in the world for more than ten years. Alcoholism, insecurity and lack of self-esteem all swarmed within him. These factors, and an overwhelming desire to rape and mutilate, combined to turn him into one of America's most heinous serial killers of all time.

FBI HIGH RISK REGISTER—JEFFREY DAHMER

1. Alcohol abuse
2. Drug abuse
3. Psychiatric history
4. Criminal history
5. Sexual problems

6. Physical abuse
7. Psychological abuse
8/9. Dominant father figure aligned with a negative relationship with male caretaker figures
10. Negative relationships with both natural mother and or adoptive mother
11. Treated unfairly
12. Head trauma
13. Demon seed

1	2	3	4	5	6	7	8/9	10	11	12	13	%
X	X	0	X	X	0	0	XX	X	0	X	?	61.5

CHAPTER 5

MYRA HINDLEY AND IAN BRADY: THE MOORS MURDERERS

"I am certain, in my mind, that if Myra Hindley had never met Ian Brady she would never have been involved with murder."

Jean Ritchie, author of *Mind of a Murderess*

IN 1966, IAN Brady and Myra Hindley were tried at Chester Assizes, England for five horrific sex murders that evoked widespread and lasting anger. At the time of writing, Brady is still serving a life sentence, while Hindley, at the age of sixty, died of respiratory failure at 4:58 p.m. on Friday, November 15, 2002, while serving her sentence.

During the final decade of her life, it has been claimed that Hindley became one of the most manipulative women held within the British penal system. She applied for parole, rediscovered her faith in Catholicism and expressed remorse for her barbaric sado-sexual crimes, writing, "I ask people to judge me as I am now and not as I was then."

From the very beginning Ian Brady knew that he was different and, as he grew older, this sense of alienation grew until one day it would consume him. Ian Duncan Stewart was born illegitimate in Glasgow on Sunday, January 2, 1938. His mother, Maggie, was a twenty-eight-year-old waitress at a local tearoom. No one ever spoke about his father, or even knew who he was. Mother and son were on their own from the start.

Soon after Ian was born, the overburdened woman moved into a tiny room in Caledonia Road, located in the heart of the tumultuous Gorbals district. This part of Glasgow has always been associated with poverty and violence, and it was in this hotbed of social deprivation that the child was raised.

Maggie found her new life with her baby increasingly difficult to maintain, and it was only a matter of time before she would be forced to give up her child. Her financial struggle, maintaining only low-paying, part-time employment, often saw the baby left at home alone while she was at work. Several months of this arrangement tipped her over the edge and she had to seriously consider what must have been a painful alternative. She decided to have Ian adopted. She made the fact known by placing an advertisement in a local shop window.

When Mary Sloan saw the card in the window, she immediately went to see Maggie Stewart. She was enchanted with the prospect of caring for a tiny baby. It helped that Mary Sloan was a kind, big-hearted lady. She explained that she would do her best for the child, and see that Ian had a happy home. Taking one look at the baby, she loved him there and then, and it was agreed that she would incorporate him into her own family. For her part, Maggie, who could not bear to lose contact with the boy altogether, was allowed to visit Ian every Sunday and would provide him with whatever clothes or toys she could afford. So aside from this early developmental blight on his existence, Ian Brady went on to live a healthy, decent childhood with the Sloans. He was fed, clothed and cared for, and he was in regular contact with that nice lady "Peggy," as Maggie had now taken to calling herself.

Ian's was not a childhood filled with the neglect, suffering and abuse that many of those around him in the slums of the Gorbals were forced to endure. In fact, even today Ian Brady himself looks back fondly on his days as a small boy, counting them as among the most joyous in his life. The only confusion he had at this early stage was that there was no one around him that he could call "mom." The Sloans never legally adopted Ian and Mrs. Sloan always insisted that Ian call her "auntie." So to Ian's mind, if she wasn't his mother and neither was "Peggy," who was?

Life in the Sloan household became increasingly unbalanced for Ian as he grew up. He was aware of his different status from the other children in the house, and was confused by Peggy's Sunday visits. People always seemed to feel sorry for him and he began to see himself as an outsider, as someone who didn't really belong. This sense of isolation from his peers would remain with him throughout his days.

A clear indication of his separateness was manifested in his behavior with other children. The boy was incredibly shy and withdrawn, and would always keep himself to himself rather than mix with others. Ian would often be found standing on his own, watching other children laugh and whoop and play their games. The child who the other kids called "Sloany" would stand perfectly still and quiet, not even attempting to join in their games.

The moment he knew his life had changed forever came at the age of nine. He had never ventured further than the bleak and dreary slums of the Gorbals. He had never been to the country, never seen a field nor a stream, when suddenly he found himself on a trip to the picturesque Loch Lomond when Mary Sloan took the whole family there for a surprise vacation. Ian was completely enraptured by the sweeping expanses of land and water, the quiet seclusion and the endless landscape. Standing atop a hill, a tremendous surge of power washed over him. In his mind, he controlled this wondrous new environment. No longer was he confined as he was in the city, stifled and unhappy amongst hundreds of other people, gray buildings and the racket of screaming citizens and traffic. Here he was completely at peace, with nothing but the rolling hills and deep waters. For the first time, he knew true freedom within this kind of isolation and the impact this experience had on him would be forever remembered.

This was the secret turning point in his life. Young Ian had tasted power, albeit in a somewhat unconventional sense, but taste it he had. He wanted more.

Back at home in the Gorbals, the images of Loch Lomond constantly pervaded his consciousness. He yearned to go back. This would be a lifelong preoccupation for Brady, this yearning for solitary interaction with his own desolate world. The physical prototype of Loch Lomond is very similar to a location favored by another serial killer, Dennis Nilsen. The rocky northern coastline of Scotland was a place where Nilsen would spend hours staring out at the water, in the same way that Brady dreamed of doing at Loch Lomond.

Soon after his visit to Loch Lomond, something unhealthy began to take root in Brady's mind. The boy began to display his new-found sense of power by snaring a cat and forcing it into a hole, which he promptly covered over with a large rock. He stood transfixed, listening to the cat meowing as it scratched and clawed at the underside of the rock in its desperation to be freed. This cruel behavior was a further extension of the control he felt he could now exercise.

Sadistic behavior toward small animals is a shared tendency with many budding psychopaths. Other multiple killers have been associated with such violence, among them the California co-ed slayer Edmund Emil Kemper III. Kemper would take pleasure in hacking cats to pieces with a knife and machete, going so far as to decapitate the family pet. He would later move on to beheading women, and this gruesome act would become this killer's homicidal signature.

It was a small step for Ian to progress on to more extreme forms of displaying his dark, new attitude.

Instead of burying cats alive, Brady moved on to throwing them off the top of tall buildings. He saw it as an amusing pastime. He knew he was different, and he knew it because he imagined he was special and far superior to the other children around him.

At the age of eleven, Ian began his schooling at Shawlands Academy. Though clearly intelligent, he was not a model pupil. He seemed to enjoy behaving in an unruly fashion. As usual, he kept himself to himself, indulging in naughty conduct on his own. But if he was out of control in the playground he was very much in control in the classroom. His handwriting was obsessively neat and he was methodical and compulsive about keeping his exercise books and school equipment in pristine condition. This was clearly his desire for order and control manifesting itself.

The next stage of Ian's development took the form of criminal behavior. He found that antisocial acts gave him a unique thrill. Ian Brady constantly experimented with more radical behavioral displays, and by the age of twelve, he had thoroughly submerged himself in the murky depths of criminality. The arrogant, aloof young loner was on a downward spiral, and moving fast. He had already begun stealing and breaking and entering nearby homes. A couple of burglaries led to him making appearances before juvenile courts. Around this time, the Sloans noted a marked decline in Ian's personality. He had become even more sullen and introverted, rejecting any form of authority and rebelling against his adoptive mother, who dealt out a number of punishments for Ian's infractions.

Brady also stopped believing in God when his pet dog died. He stayed up all night praying for the animal after it got sick. When it succumbed to its illness, Brady became an atheist overnight.

By this time, Peggy had ceased making her Sunday pilgrimages to the Sloans. Ian wondered what he had done wrong. He had suspected that she was his real mother, so why did she not want to see him? Why was his real mother not around anymore, he asked himself. This rejection by Peggy only served to enhance his feelings of not really being wanted. When he discovered that he was illegitimate, Ian's whole world collapsed. Here, finally, was confirmation of his abandonment by others. He became devastated and was angry with life in a way he had never known before.

The final straw for the young offender came shortly before his seventeenth birthday. In trouble once again, Ian this time faced a custodial sentence, as opposed to the previous occasions when he had been simply cautioned by police or placed on probation. It was decided that he would leave the Sloans, and go to live with his natural mother, who had resurfaced in Manchester. She had by this time married an Irish laborer named Pat Brady, so when Ian went to live with his new family. In December 1954, he became Ian Brady—a hate-filled loner with a bitter grudge against life.

Pat Brady quickly secured employment for his new stepson as a market errand boy. When this didn't suit him, Ian was given other jobs, as a porter and a loader. Clearly disliking his work and having no friends, Brady sank further still into his own introverted world. Already a fully emerged psychopath, he turned towards literature to fill some inner need. His choice of books is instructive. A favorite was *Mein Kampf*, Adolf Hitler's hate-filled political manifesto. Brady developed a passionate interest in the Nazis in general and Hitler in particular. Dostoevsky's *Crime and Punishment* was also devoured by Brady, with its story of a motiveless murder striking a chord within him. Needless to say, he also relished the sadistic stories of the Marquis de Sade. Books such as these gave Brady a direction in which to focus his antisocial views. The idea of sadism, and its myriad refineries, suited Ian Brady very well indeed. Finally having found an intellectual framework for his innate desire for sadistic pursuits, he was ready to strike back at the world, and he would hit hard.

Moving to Manchester failed to quell Brady's juvenile misdemeanors. Having spent different periods at reform schools and at a prison in Manchester, he was truly outraged with his life. While incarcerated, he had intentionally cultivated fellow prisoners, taking note of their varied knowledge and gleaning whatever titbits he could from the upper echelons of the criminal fraternity surrounding him. Brady had a fascination with such people and dreamed of becoming a gangster himself.

After a fight with a warden at an open reform school in Hatfield, Ian Brady was transferred to a much tougher institution at Hull. When he was freed, Brady vowed that he would become a significant criminal. His days of petty delinquencies and small-time burglaries were over. He was determined to hit the big time and leave his mark on the world. He would never make the grade as an ordinary criminal. Instead, over the next decade he would transform himself into one of the most hated figures in British history.

When Bob and Nellie Hindley conceived their daughter Myra, it was while her father was on leave from his parachute regiment. Myra was born in Gorton, an industrial district of Manchester, on Wednesday, July 23, 1942. Her mother, known within the family as Hettie, was a machinist. When the Second World War ended, Bob became a laborer.

At age four, Myra was joined by a sister, Maureen. With this new addition to the family, there was little room left in the Hindley household and Myra was sent to live with her maternal grandmother, Ellen, whom Myra came to call Granny Maybury. Myra and Granny Maybury doted on each other, and her grandmother would become one of the most important people in Myra's life. As Myra herself later revealed, she much preferred life at her grandmother's. For one thing, it saved her the considerable anxiety of having to witness her drunken father unleashing his frustrations on her mother. Nellie was the recipient of many beatings from Bob Hindley.

This kind of violence was common behavior in the neighborhood, an almost ritualized event every Saturday night as the bars emptied their inebriated men onto the streets and sent them weaving homewards to terrorize their wives and families. Myra came to deeply resent her father, who never shrunk from giving his daughter a taste of his fists if she ever interfered with one of his spousal beatings. Myra later said how she learned a lot about dominance and control from her abusive father. She also recalled loathing his thuggish antics around the home and the way this behavior permeated her entire world.

Despite her dislike for Bob Hindley and his violent ways, Myra grew up as a seemingly happy, well-adjusted young girl. She loved animals and younger children, and was thought of as a kind and gentle soul, remembered for singing a lot and playing the harmonica.

Further traumas in Myra's early years occurred when her good friend Michael Higgins died. One afternoon Michael asked her if she would like to go swimming at a local reservoir. She was unable to go. Michael went anyway and was drowned. "Myra went into a shell for a while. She was absolutely devastated that Michael had died. She wasn't the same girl for months and months after that. In fact it was a year or so...a long time," remembers her friend at the time, Elizabeth Cummings. Jean Ritchie, Myra's biographer, adds, "Myra went and visited Michael's parents, his mother all the time. And she actually converted to Catholicism. Michael had been a Catholic and she converted in the wake of his death." The psychologist Dr. David Holmes continues, "With Michael, Myra invested quite a lot, and lost quite a lot... to some degree she might have blamed herself, she also blamed everyone else, and this was the beginning of the distancing of her from other people, and also within this, she would hide in religion... another step away from humanity and a new kind of aim, and career."

This loss of Michael was followed by a slump in her academic achievements and a complete loss of interest in her schoolwork. The first chance she got, she left school and found employment as a junior clerk. Though she had always remained very fond of her grandmother, she was completely in love with Granny Maybury's dog, Duke. When Duke was hit and killed by a car, Myra's whole world collapsed. First it was the death of Michael, now Duke was gone. Myra was despondent.

The complete opposite of the cold young man she would one day collide with, Myra leaned further toward religion after the death of the pet; Brady, of course, had instantly renounced his faith when his pet dog died. Religion played an important part in Myra's early years. She had been born into Catholicism, been raised by Granny Maybury as a Protestant, and returned to the Catholic faith at the age of sixteen. She was sexually inexperienced, poorly developed emotionally—by her own admission—and was generally unadventurous. She viewed herself as a rather bland, insignificant entity, and this was aptly manifested in her decision, a year later, to become engaged to Ronnie Sinclair—a local boy who worked at the Co-op. The relationship didn't last long.

Ronnie soon bored Myra and she broke things off. She claimed that he was immature and that she disapproved of his smoking and drinking. Myra's biographer Jean Ritchie thinks that there was more to it than that. "Half the time Myra wanted the classic husband and two kids, which all the girls around her aspired to, but there was another part of her that didn't really want to do that." Ronnie, with his job at the Co-op was nothing if not conventional, and part of Myra instinctively rejected that. In the opinion of Dr. David Holmes, "Being brought up by her grandmother to have a certain sense of self-importance, Myra Hindley did require something more from life than 2.4 children and a marriage. This would not be stimulating to her. For some women, they require a certain amount of violence...a certain S&M quality to their relationship, and Myra was of this type."

Now eighteen, Myra's next boyfriend would be twenty-three-year-old Ian Brady. Boring he was not. They met when Myra began to work as a typist at the Manchester engineering firm of Millwards, where Brady was also employed. The tall, brooding loner, with his shock of hair and steely gaze caught Myra off-guard. She was instantly fascinated by him and attracted. Myra's friend Marie Cheffings remembers, "Ian was quite an attractive, handsome man, with a motorbike that everyone wanted to ride on, or look at it. I mean we were all mesmerized by it, really. There wasn't really many motorbikes in Gorton at that time."

Myra Hindley had spent her whole life waiting for someone like Ian Brady to materialize and here he was at last. Used to being dominated by her father, she was an easy target for someone like Brady. He systematically set about smashing down the boundaries of this innocent young woman. He would corrupt her thoroughly.

To catch his prey, Brady played a long game. He acted cool and stand-offish to Myra, making her come after him. Every night, she would write in her diary of her intense longing for this "enigmatic" man, a longing that would remain unfulfilled for some time. As she fluctuated from "loving him to hating him," Brady remained steadfastly disinterested for a year.

"It was that famous Christmas party, when they got together, and they became an item. From there on in, at that stage, Brady started to indoctrinate Hindley into his views on politics, life, sex, and so on," say Geoff Knupfer, former Chief Superintendent of the Greater Manchester Police. At this office Christmas party, Brady, his courage fortified with drink, asked Hindley for a date. It was to be the start of her initiation into his secret world. Their first time out was to see *The Nuremberg Trials*, a film about the Nazi war trials. Over the coming weeks, he played her records of Nazi marching songs and encouraged Myra to read some of his favorite books: *Mein Kampf, Crime and Punishment*, and the works of Marquis de Sade. Myra readily obliged. Her inexperience and hunger for Brady as a partner left her incapable of distinguishing which of her new experiences were healthy and which were not.

All the while, and unknown to Hindley, Brady was plotting to commit the ultimate act—the taking of a human life. It was something he had dreamed of often and now he had someone with whom he could share this act. As a person with no conscience at all, he had no inhibitions about committing the act nor involving someone else in it.

Myra was a virgin when she met Brady and he became her first lover. Immersed in physical and emotional desire for Brady, she readily soaked up his distorted philosophical theories. Her greatest desire was to please him. She even changed the way she dressed for him. She took to wearing tall boots, a miniskirt and bleached her hair—all to satisfy Brady's desire for a Germanic, Aryan-style woman.

As part of her new sexual adventure she allowed Brady to take pornographic photographs of her. With such a devoted audience, Brady's ideas became increasingly paranoid and outrageous. And Myra just took it all in. When

Brady told her there was no God, she stopped going to church, and when he told her that rape and murder were not wrong, that in fact murder was the "supreme pleasure," she did not question it. Her personality had become totally fused with his.

The couple played bondage games, with Brady as the aggressor and Hindley as his willing subjugate. She would be whipped and flagellated, tied up and had a hood placed over her head during sex. The more in awe she was of her overpowering partner, the more receptive she became to his extreme ideas and perversions. When Brady had corrupted her as much as he felt necessary, he was ready to indoctrinate her into his world of murder.

As we saw with Fred and Rose West, this relationship was a classic case of *folie à deux*, where one partner's dominant mentality totally eclipses the other's. Hindley had become utterly compliant to Brady's demands and when he asked her to help him kill, she complied.

One person who witnessed Brady and Hindley at their worst was David Smith, common-law husband of Myra's sister, Maureen. Smith had become a sort of friend with Brady, and together the pair planned daring criminal capers that they never quite got around to pulling off. Unknown to Smith, Brady had at one time planned to murder him but had been talked out if it by Myra, who said it would upset her sister Maureen too much.

Instead, Brady slowly drew Smith into his murderous conspiracy. Like Myra, Smith was a natural follower and Brady was their leader. Smith looked upon Brady as some sort of master criminal in the making and Smith was more than willing to come along for the ride. Smith thought he could handle it all and was a willing disciple of Brady, with his soft Scottish accent and his sharp brain.

Brady recognized in Smith a quality similar to Myra's— a willingness to be molded by a stronger personality. Smith was a valuable resource, strong and biddable and Brady felt he could use him to carry out his orders. Eventually, Brady revealed to Smith his plans to commit murder. The ever-compliant Smith indicated that he was ready to go along with it.

When the time came for Brady and Hindley to draw Smith into their murder plot, they invited him back to the house that they shared with Myra's grandmother. Brady told Smith that they could share a few drinks and Smith readily agreed. He was in no way prepared for what happened next. Left alone in the kitchen for a moment, Smith heard a thud, followed by a commotion from the living room. Then Myra called out, a trace of anxiety in her tone, "Dave, help him."

Smith rushed into the living room to find Brady standing over the writhing body of a young man, an axe in his hand. The teenager had already been struck a number of times with the weapon, judging from the amount of blood pouring from his head. As Smith watched in horror, Brady continued hacking away at the youth's face and neck. "Fucking cunt," Brady spat, "dirty little bastard," an oblique reference to the young man's sexual preferences. After a short while, the young man's screams faded away to a debilitated gurgle, which Brady quelled by thrusting a pillow over his face and smothering him, then knotting a cord tightly around his neck. Brady had smashed the boy's skull with the axe a total of fourteen times and had reduced it to pulp. An eerie silence pervaded the room. The boy was dead.

The murder committed, Brady handed the gore-streaked axe to Smith. "Feel the weight of that," he said casually. Smith took the axe, covering it in his finger-prints as Brady had planned. Myra suddenly materialized behind Smith and, after an observation from Brady as to how "this one had been the messiest yet," the couple set about cleansing the area of blood, brain tissue and bone fragment. Smith noted how they carried on with their gruesome task with about as much emotion as if they had been scrubbing their front doorstep. It struck Smith from what Brady and Hindley had said that this was not the first homicide that the pair had committed.

The corpse was then wrapped in a blanket, lashed with cord and carried upstairs. "Eddie's a dead weight," quipped Brady as they dumped the body in a spare bedroom. Myra, who had just settled her grandmother after the elderly lady had become aroused by the sudden flurry of activity from downstairs, made tea for them all in the kitchen. Smith felt his legs buckle and he flopped down into a chair, his face drained of color. He sat there, for a moment finding it very difficult to speak, as Myra placed a mug of tea before him. Slowly he turned and faced Brady sitting opposite him.

Brady stared back, with the slightest trace of a smile as Myra said, "You should have seen the look on his face, the astonishment in his eyes as you hit him." She then went on to tell Smith about how she had previously been stopped on the moors by a policeman while her partner-in-crime was burying the corpse of a murdered child.

Smith took it all in, his head spinning, trying not to panic at what he had just seen and what he was now being told. Brady had said to Smith in the midst of discussing a number of crimes he had committed, "I've killed three or four, and I'll do another one, but I'm not due for another one for three months."

The youth that lay dead in Brady and Hindley's spare bedroom was Edward Evans. Brady and Hindley had picked up the youngster at Manchester Central Station and had taken him back to the house in Wardle Brook Avenue. The seventeen-year-old boy was a homosexual and he had gone back with the pair on the understanding that sexual activity would take place between himself and Brady.

As Brady told his story, Smith listened to as much as he could before Brady turned matters around and asked him to help dispose of the body. Desperate to flee the premises at the first opportunity, Smith agreed to leave and return early the next morning with a large cart to wheel the mutilated body out of the house to Myra's car for subsequent disposal. As soon as he got home, a terrified David Smith immediately told his wife of his night of horror. They quickly agreed that he would call the police, and Smith made the call from a public telephone booth. His actions brought the bloody career of two of Britain's most hated murderers to an end. Ian Brady, the psychopathic serial killer, and his willing accomplice, Myra Hindley, would be arrested the next day and their terrible crimes exposed for all the world to see.

The murders began in 1963. Myra had taken driving lessons because Brady could only ride a motorcycle and had reasoned that if they were to abduct people, they were going to need a car. Myra did not hesitate—she threw herself into her lessons and passed her test with ease.

Their first victim was sixteen-year-old Pauline Reade. She was on her way to a dance when she was picked up by Brady and Hindley. Pauline Reade's body would not be found for another twenty-four years. Brady had led her out into the barren expanses of Saddleworth Moor, while Myra, according to a statement she gave many years later, went to find somewhere to park the car. When she returned she found that Brady had already slashed Pauline's throat. She was not yet dead but lay dying on the blackened moor as blood still pumped from her wound. Brady had also sexually assaulted Pauline. Once Pauline had died they buried her body under the damp earth.

In later years, Myra Hindley always played down her role in the murders. She was always "somewhere else" when they happened. As both Brady and Hindley were pathological liars, it is difficult to separate the truth from the reality. However, given Brady's highly dominant character, is it likely that Brady killed all their victims, with Myra aiding in their abduction and disposal.

Brady and Hindley's next victim was twelve-year-old John Kilbride, who vanished on Saturday, November 23, 1963. His brother Danny has vivid memories of John's disappearance:

John was the oldest child. He was almost twelve when he went missing. The last time I saw my brother John was in 1963, on a Saturday morning, as I got up. What I used to do every Saturday was help the market stallholders pack away. He just never came home that night. My mom rung the police, about half past six, 'cause he was always home by that time, anyway. He was always home by half past six... the police were rung, sort of thing... he was missing.

In their statement, they said that they picked him up at Ashton Market, well, Hindley had. She led John to the car. I think after a few weeks we knew he wasn't coming home. We knew he hadn't run away. We knew something had happened to him, but we didn't know what... not for two years.

When John Kilbride's body was exhumed from his shallow grave on Saddleworth Moor, police noted that his pants had been dragged down to his knees. This strongly indicated that Brady had sexually assaulted the boy before he was strangled to death and buried.

By the time of this murder, Brady and Hindley had perfected their victim-selecting technique. According to Geoff Knupfer, "The role that Myra Hindley played was always one of initial contact with the child. Sometimes Brady was absent and came along later. On other occasions, Brady came along behind on a motorcycle, flashing his headlamp, signaling: 'There is another one here, stop and talk to this individual.'" This method worked. On the night of Monday, June 16, 1964, twelve-year-old Keith Bennett fell into the couple's clutches. Keith had been walking over to his grandmother's house and his route led him along Westmoreland Street where Brady and Hindley were living at the time.

It appears that they snatched the boy from the pavement as he passed by the house. Keith Bennett's body has never been found. Both Hindley and Brady have admitted burying the boy on Saddleworth Moor, but despite concerted efforts including the assistance of Brady and Hindley themselves, the police were never able to locate his grave. Winnie Johnson, Keith Bennett's mother, is painfully aware of what Brady and Hindley put her son through. She states, "[Brady] hit Keith on the back of the head, knocked him out, put a machine cord rubber around his throat, and broke his neck. He actually assaulted him afterwards and left his clothes beside where they buried him... he didn't know he was going to his death." Given her own terrible personal involvement in the case, Winnie Johnson's verdict on a fitting punishment for Brady and Hindley was understandable: "I would put them in a big enough hole to bury both of them, throw the soil on top of them and bury them alive. 'Cause, that's all they need. 'Cause, those kind of people are not worth the salt of the earth."

The penultimate murder of Brady and Hindley's career is possibly the most shocking. Ten-year-old Lesley Ann Downey was abducted from a fairground on the day after Christmas, 1964. She was taken to 16 Wardle Brook Avenue, where Brady and Hindley were lodging with Myra's grandmother. Taken to an upstairs room in the house, Lesley Ann was forced to strip naked, keeping just her shoes and socks on, and pose for Brady to take some photographs. She appears in these heartbreaking photographs, gagged with a scarf and looking confused and frightened.

In a terrible twist, Brady also made tape recordings of the terrified girl's pleas to be released. To an insane background of Christmas carols, Lesley can be heard begging to leave because her mother will be worried about her. She is also heard asking Brady to take his hands off her. At several points she cries out, "Don't undress me, will you?"

Geoff Knupfer, the former Chief Superintendent of Greater Manchester Police, elaborates, "[Hindley's] voice is heard on the tape, telling the little girl to be quiet, because clearly she was very distressed indeed. Hindley was very worried at the time that the neighbors would hear the little girl crying, and that was the concern." Hindley's biographer, Jean Ritchie, adds another distressing detail: "Lesley Ann Downey was pleading with Hindley, 'Please Mom'—she calls her 'Mom' all the way through it—so by appealing to Myra's maternal instincts she might make these awful things stop. But Myra is gagging her, so we don't know what abuse happened. Myra claimed that there was no sexual abuse—there probably was. The next day they took Lesley up to the moor and buried her."

In the words of Dr. David Holmes, "The killing of Lesley Ann Downey marked a significant change in the killing career of Myra Hindley. [It showed that she had] the confidence to actually kill somebody within feet and inches of neighbors, rather than out on the moors."

At his trial for murder, Brady was questioned about the tape by Elwyn Jones, leading the case for the prosecution. "Why did you keep it all that time?" he asks. "Because it was unusual," was Brady's casual reply.

Elwyn pressed him futher. "Is that the best adjective you can apply, Brady?"

The defendant was unrepentant. "Yes, that is the best adjective I can find at the moment."

Elwyn tried again, "For those interested in perversion and horror it was something of a connoisseur's piece, was it not?"

Brady refused to take the bait. "I wouldn't know," he replied. But Brady did know. He knew all about perversion and he knew all about horror.

Police later recovered a suitcase from a locker at Manchester railway station. The case contained pornographic images of Lesley Ann, the tape recordings, coshes, wigs and plans and documents pertinent to a number of crimes. It was Brady's gruesome souvenir collection.

Monster that he certainly is, Ian Brady is also a highly intelligent man. As a young man, adrift in a world he could never truly feel a part of, his natural creativity and intelligence was instead channeled into destruction.

Like so many youngsters who go on to become serial killers, Brady preferred his own company. He was a frustrated loner who existed in his own fantasy land, an individual who stayed on the sidelines, aware that he could never belong to groups of children of his own age. He has told of how he would walk through dark streets late at night, passing by houses with the warm glows of domesticity emanating from their windows. He told of how he felt comforted by being alone and outside of these cosy family scenes. It is difficult to imagine a more lonely and isolated scenario and offers a stark indicator of just how detached Brady had become from the rest of society.

With no one to call "dad," we know that he suffered the social stigma of knowing he was illegitimate. Perhaps even more significantly, having bonded with his sole parent as a baby, he was then abandoned by her. Psychologists and social scientists have demonstrated that parental abandonment can have a traumatizing effect on babies and that the earliest months of a child's development are key times for creating a mother-and-baby bond. With Brady, that bond was severed just as it began to form. Ian Brady may have recovered from this early psychological trauma had his mother disappeared forever. But she didn't—she returned to visit him on a regular weekly basis for many years. This was a constant reminder to him each week of parental betrayal.

Adoption and being brought into an entirely different home with different faces at such a tender age can cause immense emotional upheaval to a developing personality. We believe it was at this point that Brady's mental blueprint was sealed. Although the Sloans, well-intentioned as they were, became his family, it was on a superficial level only. Brady was part of the family but also left in no doubt that he was an outsider, too.

When the Sloan family visited Loch Lomond, Ian discovered something that he was immediately at one with. Something stirred in him—perhaps the mix of inner loneliness combined with the isolation of the terrain, the beauty of the landscape and large expanses of water, now fused.

Many psychologically healthy youngsters develop artistic and literary roots from such experiences. Ian, however, not having enjoyed healthy, formative years, turned these experiences into something less positive. He turned in on himself and became a brooding youth, jealous of his peers and slowly seething. The need to commit criminal acts can easily spring from such seeds.

Many emerging psychopaths and sexual sadists have juvenile histories of cruelty to animals. Edmund Kemper, mentioned before, hacked cats into pieces, while Arthur Shawcross threw kittens into water, allowing them to struggle to shore before repeatedly throwing them back until the creatures drowned. Ian Brady was no exception here when he started to take out his adolescent frustrations on cats, hurling them off high buildings or burying them alive.

This sickening behavior has its foundations in the young offender's mind as he struggles with a need to inflict pain and suffering on his peers, but is unable to do so. It is the thought processes that are important here. In early adolescence, Brady developed this desire to inflict harm. When he did finally develop the ability to murder other human beings, it is significant that he tended to choose children of a certain age—the same age as the children around him that he despised and ignored when he first became aware that he was "different" from them. It was as though he was venting his adolescent rage as an adult.

Ian Brady's intelligence was another important factor. Unlike a more intellectually limited killer, such as Fred West, Brady was able to apply some sort of intellectual framework to his actions. His reading directly fed into his acts. His obsessions with Adolf Hitler and the Nazis gave him an historical precedent for superior beings "justifiably" taking the lives of their inferiors, while his passion for the writings of Dostoevsky, whose philosophies he built his life around, gave him his twisted moral core. Never mind that his love of Dostoevsky was based on an imperfect or skewed understanding of the great Russian author, Brady took from his works what fitted in with his own unusual worldview. Dostoevsky's great novel *Crime and Punishment*, which meant so much to Brady, was intended by the author as a tale of redemption—a young, disturbed man kills an old woman simply because the opportunity presents itself to him. Subsequently captured and imprisoned, the young man embarks on a path to redemption as he comes to terms with his actions and seeks forgiveness from society and from God. For Brady, the opportunistic killing was the key element of the story. The rest meant nothing to him.

Indeed, rather than seek forgiveness from God like Raskolnikov, the protagonist of *Crime and Punishment*, Brady actively rejected religious belief from an early age. This carried through to his criminal career. On one occasion, he actually screamed obscenities to heaven while standing over the body of a murdered child.

With Myra Hindley, her formative years were different. Although she scores higher on the FBI's High Risk Register than Ian Brady, we are confident she would probably never have killed had she not met Brady. She was an empty vessel into which Brady poured his psychotic fantasies. Indeed, there is some doubt whether Hindley ever actually committed the act of murder itself.

Despite the problems Myra Hindley suffered as a child and into her early teens, her adolescent history was no different to millions of other girls who never commit a crime in their lives. With one previous boyfriend to Brady, we can even suggest that until she met Brady she was a thoroughly decent, if naïve, person. It is not too difficult to imagine why at eighteen the rather drab Myra was attracted to the tall, mysterious and well-read Ian Brady.

But if we can argue that Myra would probably never have killed without Brady's influence, how do we account for the fact that her High Risk Register score is almost double that of her partner in crime? It is certainly the case that Brady would have gone on to become a killer with or without Hindley's help, but not vice versa. Is Myra the exception that proves the rule? An anomaly? Probably not.

It is a well-accepted fact that female serial killers who murder children are extremely rare. We also know that Brady raped all of his victims, while Myra Hindley did not. The maternal impulse not to murder children is extremely powerful, and seems to have been present in Hindley, too. Her case may be indicative of something quite different. Despite Hindley's much higher High Risk Register score, it can plausibly be argued that the female psyche is simply more tolerant of the negative effects that comprise the FBI's thirteen risk factors that indicate serial killer tendencies. Women, put simply, may be more emotionally resilient than men, and thus, are able to withstand a greater degree of emotional and physical abuse than men are. As a result, they are less prone to become serial killers.

FBI HIGH RISK REGISTER—
IAN BRADY AND MYRA HINDLEY:

1. Alcohol abuse
2. Drug abuse
3. Psychiatric history
4. Criminal history
5. Sexual problems
6. Physical abuse
7. Psychological abuse
8/9. Dominant father figure aligned with a negative relationship with male caretaker figures
10. Negative relationships with both natural mother and or adoptive mother
11. Treated unfairly
12. Head trauma
13. Demon seed

Ian Brady

1	2	3	4	5	6	7	8/9	10	11	12	13	%
0	0	0	X	0	0	0	00	X	0	0	?	15

Myra Hindley

1	2	3	4	5	6	7	8/9	10	11	12	13	%
0	0	0	0	0	X	X	XX	0	0	0	?	30.77

CHAPTER 6

JOHN ALLEN MUHAMMAD AND LEE BOYD MALVO: THE WASHINGTON SNIPERS

"The low point of the investigation? We did not know what to do to stop them. These two individuals were cold-blooded murderers. They didn't care who they killed...The high point of the investigation? Catching them."

Sergeant Roger Thomson, Lead Investigator,
Montgomery County Police

IT IS ALMOST impossible to convey in written words the degree of terror the Washington Snipers inflicted upon their community. For days, the entire city was gripped by fear. A man innocently mowing his lawn is shot; a child on his way to school is gunned down; a gas station attendant takes a bullet while pumping gas; a woman reading a book on a shopping center bench is assassinated with a high velocity shot to the head. The violence is indiscriminate and random. No one can guess when and who the killers will shoot next. Imagine knowing that you could be murdered by simply stepping outside your front door. This is how the people of Washington, D.C. felt during those terrifying few days in October 2002.

A casual visitor to Washington, D.C. during those days would have seen some unusual sights, because people were kneeling next to their cars as they filled them with gas, or running, weaving, from their vehicles and into their houses or shops. They were all trying to escape the attentions of the Washington Snipers. Most succeeded; some failed.

The Washington Snipers were forty-one-year-old John Allen Muhammad and his accomplice, seventeen-year-old Lee Boyd Malvo. If their paths had never crossed, would they have murdered so many, or were they born to kill?

Many of the killings took place just north of Washington, D.C. in Montgomery County, Maryland, a community of about one million residents. The people who live here enjoy above-average incomes and a significant portion of them are senators, congressmen and executives of large corporations. The homicide rate in this affluent suburb was around nineteen to twenty deaths per year, compared to the 100-200 murders committed annually in the poorer parts of the city. Montgomery County was simply not prepared for the level of violence that the Washington Snipers were to inflict upon it. By the time the killers were captured, fifteen people were dead and twenty-three had been wounded, all shot from a distance by a high-powered rifle without conscience or prejudice. The victims were young and old, back and white, male and female.

When the killings began, the local police went into panic mode. 911 calls flooded in and the emergency services were overwhelmed. The police department ran out of personnel and reinforcements had to be drafted in from other states.

Supervising Sergeant Roger Thomson, a police officer for thirty-two years, including twenty-three years as a homicide detective, gave an exclusive interview for *How to Make a Serial Killer*. He described the developing events as "surreal," adding:

> You were there, with all these people, and no one knew what to do next to protect the public. It was a problem for the executive staff. We were talking about kids at schools and people in shopping centers, and how are we going to protect them. It was very, very concerning to everyone involved. So we had a lot of things that had to go on at the same time. We had to have briefings on what we had, we had to put investigators all over the place, to try to find evidence and witnesses. And we also had the patrol division who had to do some kind of protection for the people in the area. Within days, there were over 1,000 officers on the case. We had them coming from everywhere, even feeding them and putting them into hotels was a nightmare. Even the community brought in food to feed them. It was a great community effort.

Ordinary Americans feared for their lives. They became too frightened to put gas in their cars or let their children play outdoors. For twenty-three horrific days a series of random sniper killings terrorized Washington, D.C. A walk down the street became a gamble with life and death. Jon Ward of the *Washington Times* explains, "I think people began to be scared when they realized that the shootings were random... you had to come to grips with the fact that someone could be pointing a gun at you as you sat in your car. They were just picking people at random. If you were out there, where they could get to you, you were gone."

Lee Malvo was born in Kingston, Jamaica, on Monday, February 18, 1985, to Una James and Leslie Malvo. His childhood was not always a happy one. Dr. Dewey Cornell was Malvo's court-appointed psychologist, and spent fifty-three hours with Malvo, trying to understand his motivation. He says:

In many ways, Lee's childhood was the perfect storm of what was to come. He was treated very abusively by his mother, who insisted he obey her. She would beat him if he was disrespectful... if he didn't do a good job of washing the dishes, or doing his chores, then she left him. She left him repeatedly to take jobs in other places and would come in, move him to other homes when she couldn't pay the bills and then would disappear again. And each time this happened, there was a mixture of stress, anger, distress and resentment. He threatened to kill himself to try to convince her to stay with him.

Throughout his childhood, teachers, neighbors—many people—observed how this little boy desperately needed a father figure.

Malvo's partner-in-crime was twenty-four years his senior. Born Sunday, December 31, 1950, in the "Big Easy," New Orleans, John Williams changed his name to John Muhammad when he converted to Islam in the mid-1980s.

Muhammad had been deeply affected by his mother dying when he was very young. He was often picked on by other children and relatives when he was a kid. He went through his entire life feeling that his potential had never been recognized and that, had it been, his life would have been much happier and more successful. In short, he blamed other people for his failures in life.

John married Mildred, his second wife, in 1988. Those who knew him thought him to be a good husband and father. Roger Holmes is a mechanic who met John in 1985, during their stints in the Army at Fort Lewis. Holmes recalls Muhammad's domestic set-up: "Everybody thought it was the perfect family. They got married and "Little John" was born first and subsequently two daughters. He was always a womanizer, but at the same time he always took care of his family. I'd say he was a disciplinarian. It wasn't like an abuse streak, you know... more like nurturing. I never saw John yell at his children. If there was something he felt they hadn't done right, he would talk to them." Indeed, many who knew John spoke highly of his treatment of his children, who were always very respectful.

For most of his married life, John Muhammad was a combat engineer in the National Guard. When he was away he desperately missed his children, in fact, he didn't like being in the military at all. It was something he was committed to doing and it provided a living for his family. He was highly trained, and had learned how to fire a weapon and was skilled in sniper tactics. He had also seen battle experience in the Gulf War. When John returned home from the conflict, his wife claimed that she saw a change in him, that he had become a darker, much more serious person. He may even have suffered from some sort of neurological damage from chemicals used during the conflict, though this is a difficult claim to substantiate.

On leaving the military, John began to feel bitter against his country and the Army. This would soon turn to resentment towards his wife. Roger Holmes recalls, "There was a point when he changed. I mean he looked the same, and he was pretty much the same, but there was something about him that just wasn't the John I had come to know." John Muhammad became increasingly unpredictable, charming one minute, menacing the next. The John his friends knew was different to the man Mildred saw at home. Behind closed doors he dropped any pretence of normality. He routinely threatened Mildred and she rapidly came to believe that John had the capacity to kill her.

When her fear of John became too much to bear, Mildred left him. John was furious. He tracked Mildred down and literally kidnapped his kids, taking them to the Caribbean, where he was earning money forging fake documents.

It was while working as a forger in Jamaica that John Muhammad first came into contact with Lee Malvo. Lee's mother was desperate to move to the United States and turned to John Muhammad for help. In the meantime, she introduced John to her teenage son, Lee. A bond soon formed between the two males. Lee, especially, saw in John the father figure he needed. According to Lee Malvo's court-appointed clinical psychologist, Dr. Dewy Cornell, "When John Muhammad came along, to Lee he seemed liked the perfect father, because here was a man who was taking care of his own three children, was a single parent, seemed very dedicated to the welfare of his children and John treated Lee with the type of respect and honesty that no one else did." John Muhammad's powerful influence would soon change Lee Malvo's life forever.

While John was in the Caribbean, back in the U.S. Mildred was frantically trying to track down her missing children. When John was finally located, the children were forcibly removed from him and taken back to America. A custody hearing date was set for September 4, 2001. John went along, thinking he would be able to tell his side of the story. Instead, he was stunned to find that the court was not interested in anything he had to say. The hearing was simply called to formally return his children to the custody of their mother.

The audio records from the court hearing make for enlightening reading:

John: Can you please tell me exactly what is going on, here?

Judge: There is a parenting plan that was entered by the Court on October 6, 2000 last year.

John: I am aware of it... the children were never mentioned.

Judge: According to the Court record, by the mother...

John: Are you telling me the reason why I don't have my children, won't be able to keep my children, is because I don't have the proper paperwork in?

Judge: The order says that the mother has sole full residential and placement care of the children. You do have an opportunity to express your side of the story, for the court to hear it, all right?

John: So, uh, uh, ah, I am not, uh, able to see my children?

Judge: Your visitation is suspended.

The outcome of the court hearing left John reeling. He couldn't accept that he wouldn't be able to see his children again. Unable to take in the judge's decision, he sought further legal advice, turning to family lawyer John Mills, who agreed to take on his case. Mills says, "[John] was a very normal, concerned father, who was disturbed by what had gone on in court. He didn't understand what had gone on in court, but when I explained it to him he was perfectly willing to work within the system, expecting that we could all get it straightened out and organized again."

But the effect of the judge's decision would not only change John's life—it would end the lives of twenty-three other people. The decision left John at his lowest ebb. According to John's attorney, John Mills, "It's sad that the people would die, their lives would be destroyed, and their families' lives destroyed. And the judge's decision was probably what pushed John over the edge."

Now living in the seaport town of Bellingham, Washington State, depressed and brooding, John started to think of revenge. At the same time, he saw in Lee Malvo someone who needed a father figure and someone he could teach and mold to help him to exact the revenge he wanted. John had vowed vengeance on his ex-wife, but how far would he be prepared to go? After searching for Mildred for four months, John Muhammad tracked her down to the Washington, D.C. area. Now he could carry out his plan.

As a first step, Muhammad began to indoctrinate Lee Malvo into the use of firearms. He also persuaded him to enroll at Bellingham High School, where Lee turned out to be a fairly standard student. He was an excellent artist but beyond that was unremarkable. Classmate Chrissy Greenawalt remembers Lee well. "He was very, very friendly but not necessarily an extrovert. He didn't really try to make friends, and wasn't about to give details of his life."

Both John and Lee lived with Earl Dancy, who recalls John as being "very manipulative... he gained your confidence, he gained your trust. Once he conquered your confidence, he took advantage." Dancy also witnessed a change in Lee Malvo's character. "He was always angry, mad. I would expect any teenager to be like that, but he had a lot of anger in him for no reason at all."

Lee's education gradually became more than just schoolwork. Every day after class, John would teach Lee how to shoot at the local gun range, and John became obsessed with the boy's marksmanship. In time, Lee became a dead shot.

John wanted Lee to learn as much as he could about guns. He also encouraged him to watch films such as *The Matrix* and to play "shoot 'em up" and sniper computer games. Experts would later conclude that these types of activities desensitized a young and impressionable Lee to the events that he later took part in.

As part of their make-believe military training, John and Lee adopted a strict daily training routine of exercise and limited diet. They forced themselves to eat just one meal a day, consisting of just water, honey and crackers.

On Saturday, February 16, 2002, two days before Malvo's seventeenth birthday, John Muhammad gave the teenager his first big test. John was angry with a female friend of his ex-wife who had given testimony at the custody hearing and sent his apprentice out to kill her. Neither John nor Lee knew that the woman's twenty-one-year-old niece, Keina Cook, would be at home. When Keina, instead of the intended victim, opened the door to Lee, he shot her in the face. It was the wrong woman, but he had made his first kill nonetheless.

From February to October 2002, the two men ricocheted around the U.S., robbing and killing people as their needs or desires demanded. Eventually, they turned up in the Washington, D.C. area and prepared to launch one of the worst shooting sprees in American history.

Muhammad and Malvo would drive the streets until they found a possible target. Once they were in position, Muhammad would keep watch from the driver's seat while Malvo climbed into the back, lifted up the rear seat and took up position in the 1989 dark blue Chevrolet Caprice's trunk. A hole had been cut in the bodywork, through which a gun barrel could be pointed.

Their first victim, fifty-five-year-old James Martin, was killed by a single bullet as he walked across a supermarket parking lot in Wheaton, Maryland, just north of Washington. They struck again on the morning of Thursday, October 3, 2002. The Washington rush hour was reaching its height with all the major highways on the 62-mile beltway circling the capital full of cars containing people going to work. The first target of the day was a landscaper, thirty-nine-year-old James "Sonny" Buchanan. At 7:31 a.m., Buchanan was mowing grass by the side of a road. Some distance away, Malvo watched him through his Remington Bushmaster rifle's sight scope. At Muhammad's command, Malvo fired. Buchanan was hit but managed to stagger down the sidewalk and into a parking lot, where he collapsed in front of two employees. The bullet had struck between his left shoulder blade and his spine. He was rushed to a hospital but died a few hours later. Buchanan's sister Vickie Snider described him as a generous man. "He was my youngest brother. He was my best friend, and we were confidants. He just had a love for life, for people. This is like a nightmare, one that you never wake up from."

The snipers struck again at 8:12 a.m. the same day, while fifty-four-year-old Indian taxi driver Premkumar Walekar was pumping gas at a Mobil station in Aspen Hill, Maryland, also just north of Washington, D.C. Malvo downed Walekar with a single shot fired from the other side of a six-lane highway. A doctor on the scene tried to revive the victim but it was no use. The .223 caliber bullet had ripped through Walekar's heart and lung. He died at the scene.

Twenty-five minutes later Sarah Ramos, a thirty-four-year-old housekeeper and nanny, was shot dead as she sat quietly on a bench outside a post office in Silver Spring, Maryland. She was reading a book and waiting for her boss to pick her up. She was killed by a single shot fired by Malvo from up to 300 feet away. The bullet passed through Ramos and shattered a plate glass window. Their day's work unfinished, Muhammad and Malvo then singled out twenty-five-year-old Lori Ann Lewis. At 9:58 a.m. she was shot as she vacuumed her car at a Shell gas station in Kensington, Maryland.

Realizing that a serial killer was running amok, one of the first things police executive staff did was contact all of the schools' security staff in the area and arrange for them to get the kids who were out on recess back inside school buildings. However, there was also some concern that the killer would start to pick off officers at schools as they tried to ensure the safety of pupils. It did not take long for a feeling of paranoia to creep in.

Officers now had to ask some searching questions. Was this a terrorist situation? Were the victims and their killer connected? On that first morning nothing was known about the perpetrators and the police were forced to work completely in the dark. As a first step, they pleaded with the public to help them. Seventy-thousand phone calls and 2,000 emails poured in and the police found themselves unable to cope. Federal agents were summoned and a special FBI computer program was activated in order to help process and organize information. All of this was happening as the shootings were still going on. It was a chaotic and intense scene.

At 9:30 p.m., the next day the killers struck again. Pascal Charlot, a seventy-two-year-old Haitian-American carpenter, was shot dead in northeast Washington as he walked down the street. The local population was thrown into panic once more as they realized that the killers were just getting started. The police were confounded. They had no answers to give the shattered community. "We just did not know what to do. We did not prepare for what happened that morning," says Sergeant Roger Thomson.

Children were locked in their classrooms and told not to go near the windows. There were no outside activities; field trips were canceled, and sporting events were called off. Life had come to a halt. The Chief of Police went on television to say, "Your children are not safe anywhere, at any time." Speaking exclusively for *How to Make a Serial Killer*, Sergeant Roger Thomson explains, "The random shootings, the killers going from jurisdiction to jurisdiction, left people terrified of being able to complete even the most mundane daily tasks, such as buying gas. As soon as they knew that someone was being shot at one gas station and then at another gas station, people did all sorts of things to prevent being shot. They would go back in their car when the gas was going in... they would hide behind the car and look around to make sure that nobody was going to shoot at them."

As it turned out, the citizens of Washington, D.C., Maryland and Virginia had good reason to be scared. The killings soon came thick and fast.

October 4, at 2:30 p.m.: A forty-three-year-old woman is seriously wounded in a shopping mall parking lot in Fredericksburg, Virginia, about 50 miles southwest of Washington.

October 7, at 8:09 a.m.: A thirteen-year-old boy is hit by a bullet to the chest and seriously wounded as he gets out of his parents' car to go to the Benjamin Middle School in Bowie, Maryland, northeast of Washington.

October 9, at 8:18 p.m.: Dean Harold Meyers, fifty-three, is shot dead as he fills his car at a gas station in Manassas, Virginia, southwest of Washington.

October 11, at 9:40 a.m.: Kenneth Bridges, fifty-three, returning to his home in Philadelphia, Pennsylvania, stops at a gas station near Fredericksburg, Virginia. He is shot by a single bullet.

October 14, at 9:19 p.m.: Linda Franklin, forty-seven, is shot and killed as she loads purchases from a Home Depot hardware store into her car at a shopping center in Falls Church, Virginia, in the suburbs west of Washington. The bullet blasted into her head and she died instantly.

And so it went on. But how did the police finally track down the suspects? To begin with, they investigated every shooting in the Washington, D.C. area and found their first lead. A short time before the snipers began their rampage a liquor store was held up and two employees were shot. Police believed that there may have been a link between this crime and the ongoing shootings. Malvo's fingerprints had been found at the scene and police were able to identify them since Malvo already had a criminal record after being arrested as an illegal immigrant. His address was given as the Light House Mission, Bellingham, Washington State, where he lived with Muhammad, so the police now had two suspects.

Meanwhile, Muhammad's old army friend Roger Holmes was following the case with extra interest. He knew that two men had to be involved—one as the spotter, the other the shooter. He also knew that Muhammad was with Malvo. In what proved to be one of the most difficult decisions of his life, he phoned the FBI. He says, "They called me in and started asking me questions. They asked why I thought it was John, and why was he on the East Coast. I told them that his ex-wife lived in the D.C. area, then it took off from there."

Although the police were now closing in on the suspects, Muhammad and Malvo were still killing innocent members of the public. On October 19, at 8:00 p.m., they killed a thirty-seven-year-old man as he walked across a restaurant parking lot with his wife in Ashland, Virginia. Next up was Conrad Johnston, a local bus driver. During Muhammad and Malvo's reign of terror, Conrad had taken the extra effort to escort one of his elderly regular passengers on and off his bus to reassure her that she was safe. On the morning of October 22, he was shot as he stood on the steps of his bus, just about to start his run. It was still dark and the only lights to be seen were those inside his vehicle. He was an easy target. A gunshot rang out from the woods and Conrad was hit, staggering back into the bus's aisle as the bullet tore through his liver. A terrified passenger called for an ambulance. Conrad was rushed to the hospital for emergency surgery but died on the operating table.

Conrad was married with two young children. His sister described him as "a very gentle person. I called him 'The Gentle Giant,' because he was a big guy and very kind. He was very gentle. A loving, family man. It was a sad morning when I got the call that Conrad had been shot, and I just knew it was the sniper. About forty minutes later, the doctors came out and told us that he did not make it. And that's one day I never want to relive. That was the saddest day of my life. We went upstairs to the morgue, and when I saw him laying there, Oh, God, it was very, hard...very hard."

The murder of Conrad Johnston proved to be the Washington Snipers' final killing. The police had finally caught up with them.

A warrant for the arrest of Muhammad and Malvo was issued at 7:54 p.m. on October 24. At 12:05 a.m. a press conference was called and police released the license plate number of the snipers' car: New Jersey NDA 21Z.

That same day, a truck driver in Myersville, Maryland, heard the news and wrote down the plate number and, by an amazing stroke of luck, actually saw the car. The police acted swiftly. Officers sped to the scene and SWAT teams were drafted in by helicopter. A ring of steel was erected around the car and the enforcement officers moved in. Muhammad and Malvo were found to be sleeping in the vehicle and were arrested without a struggle at 3:15 a.m., just yards away from the I-75 highway.

For the families of the victims, knowing that the two men responsible were in custody helped their grieving process. For society at large, the arrests meant that it was safe to walk the streets again. Sonia Wells, Conrad Johnston's mother, recalls, "It's very surreal, like living in a tunnel, and you're going through the motions wondering what is going to happen next. You know, I think the biggest relief, for all of us, was when they were caught."

What was it that turned these two men into cold-blooded, hard-hearted killers? For people who knew Muhammad and Malvo, it was a hard fact to accept. Malvo's school friend Chrissy Greenawalt recalls, "I was watching the news one day, and they said they had caught them. And I don't think I saw his face, they just said his name. I thought 'Wow, how do I know that name, Lee Malvo... it's not a common name' and I just kept thinking, 'Where do I know that from?' Then it all clicked in my head, and I thought, 'Oh! My Gosh. This cannot be happening. How weird is that... our little tiny corner of the world, this guy was in my class, and he's killed fifteen people.'"

With the two killers locked up, police evidence technicians searched their car and uncovered vital circumstantial evidence. Detective Ralph Daigneau of Prince William County Police says, "Some of the evidence collected from the vehicle at the time of the arrest, for instance, was the Sony Vaio computer located by the front seat of the car. And there were several items that worked with the computer. They had a solar charger—I don't know how well it worked—and they had logs which kept track of the areas that they felt were important, areas they had scouted out as strong, possible areas, where they could wreak the most havoc."

Police also found maps marking not only where people had been shot, but also where they planned future killings. There were lots of bags of clothing and vitamins that the two ascetic killers took to keep up their health levels. The most vital piece of evidence—the murder weapon—was found hidden behind the car's back seat. It was a high-powered rifle, a Bushmaster .223 with a spot scope. It was the civilian version of the five-round Remington AR-15 military rifle Muhammad knew so well. This was an essential find, and ballistics experts would later link it to at least eleven of the shootings. Malvo's DNA was also found on the rifle.

The killers' PC, log books, maps and other items all demonstrated that the murders exhibited a high degree of planning. Clinical psychologist Dr. Evan Nelson explained the reasoning behind this type of preparedness: "All of this shows extraordinary planning. They were very careful to set themselves up for shooting in ways they could make a quick and rapid exit. They even came back to visit the scenes while the police were investigating them. This shows an amazing degree of calculation, an awareness of the wrongfulness of what they were doing in order to avoid detection. And even a willingness to flirt with the possibility of being caught, because of that sense of supremacy that they wouldn't get caught."

John Muhammad was examined by court-appointed psychiatrists, but the findings were never admitted as evidence in court. Consequently, his motivations for murder will never truly be known. Much has been made of the fact that Muhammad and Malvo left messages at scenes of shootings demanding $10 million from the American government to make the killings cease. Was money their main motivation? It certainly seems that way, but there is strong circumstantial evidence for other factors coming into play, too.

There is speculation that Muhammad wanted to kill his wife in order to get his children back. There is no hard evidence to support this, but the fact that he chose as his hunting ground the Washington, D.C. area, where Mildred lived, may not be coincidental. More pertinently, was Muhammad's losing custody of his children to his wife the trigger that initiated this tragic series of events? In the opinion of Muhammad's friend Roger Holmes, "It wasn't like he was a bad character, and that all of his life he had been doing dirty things and bad deeds. It's just that you reach your breaking point and you don't know how you will react. John went over the edge and this is the end result." Despite this insight, it is still not clear why Muhammad deliberately set out to convince a seventeen-year-old boy to take part in his mission.

While John Muhammad's motivations may be impossible to trace, much less confirm, Lee Malvo's reasons for taking part in the killings are even more difficult to fathom. In the words of his psychologist Dr. Evan Nelson, "I have evaluated, literally, close to 200 capital murder defendants, and about 400 murder defendants overall. Mr. Malvo is in a class unto his own. This is because of intellect, verbal skills, and because of the fact that he did this killing in tandem, in such a purposeful way, and that's really different to the killers we see that are impulsive, whose crimes grow out of being drunk and high, perhaps sexually aroused, or being greedy. If somebody wants something in that moment, they commit murder and then they regret it."

Dr. Dewy Cornell agrees that Malvo may have had a complex of reasons for doing what he did. "Nobody becomes a serial killer, or criminal, for just one reason. I know there is a lot of debate about nature vs. nurture, but even if you ask the question 'nature or nurture?' you are really asking the wrong question. It is always nature *and* nurture."

But perhaps Malvo's former classmate, Chrissy Greenawalt, summed Lee up better than most. "At that age, and I'm not much older than Lee, you just want to please the adults around you. You want to do well in all things... because you are trying to be a grown-up yourself, and you want to be accepted by adults. I can completely see why, because Muhammad was a caretaker and Lee had nobody else to take care of him."

Lee told his psychologist that if he wanted to understand him, he should watch the film *The Matrix*. In the movie, Keanu Reeves' character is chosen by an older, charismatic mentor to lead a revolution against an evil regime that has enslaved humanity. Lee clearly saw himself as someone fighting against the system and that is one reason why he identified with Reeves's character, Neo. For a young, idealistic and insecure seventeen-year-old such as Lee, the film's frame of reference was one he could readily buy into. This theory has been supported by Dr. Dewy Cornell. "There is pretty strong evidence that repeated exposure to entertainment violence desensitizes young people and makes them more likely to think that committing violence is an acceptable way to solve problems."

Police investigators pour scorn on this theory put forward by the defense in mitigation for Malvo's crimes. One of the senior detectives on the case, who wishes to remain anonymous, offers this alternative hardline view: "This was something that was made up. They may have played the computer games, especially Malvo. We don't have anything that shows that this is what they did all the time. That they were crazed by it. They were living in YMCAs. They were not playing video games in there. I don't think that had anything to do with it. When Malvo was talking about something like that, they grasped onto it as some kind of defense. He was brainwashed. He was involved in some kind of deadly game, like *The Matrix*, like the movie, and that sort of thing. They had to grasp onto something.

"You have two people, who killed all these people, cold-bloodedly, for no reason, maybe money. How do you defend people like that? There was so much evidence against them. Malvo had to come up with something to persuade a jury; something else was moving, causing them to do these murders. All of us know that a conscious individual, who has any kind of soul, any kind of heart, doesn't kill indiscriminately. Only terrorists do that."

While it is difficult to dismiss the police officer's views entirely, his terrorist analogy does raise an interesting point that works against his argument. Like the followers of Osama bin Laden, Lee Malvo was systematically indoctrinated by John Muhammad into his belief system.

Throughout his interrogations, Lee repeated political statements regarding the need to overthrow society. It is unlikely that these were his own views but were expressions parroting the beliefs of John Muhammad. In this way, we can argue that Lee Malvo was John Muhammad's disciple.

So does this mean that Malvo would not have killed had he not met Muhammad? Those closest to the police investigation disagree. When asked the question, Sergeant Roger Thomson emphatically replies, "No! No! Malvo should have been sentenced to death with Muhammad. I believe that. There was no brainwashing at all. We have witnesses that actually put them apart. We know where Muhammad is by himself. Malvo had every opportunity to leave. He tried to leave. He tried to get out of whatever was going on down in Louisiana... is that just him talking, or his family talking? But when you shoot somebody in the face with a .45 and then start picking people off from a distance with a sniper's rifle when there is no connection, no emotional connection, it didn't matter to me."

Dr. Evan Nelson agrees. "In my opinion, it wasn't brainwashing. This is a case of a young man eager to learn things, and an older man who is eager to teach. So, I think young Mr. Malvo found somebody whom he could idolize and adore, and choose to follow, as compared to being brainwashed."

Even though Lee Malvo was just seventeen at the time of the shootings, he still faced the death penalty. However, his defense attorney managed to convince the jury that Malvo had, in fact, been indoctrinated by Muhammad and that he was not a natural-born killer.

Malvo was spared the death penalty and was sentenced to life imprisonment instead.

Dr. Dewy Cornell has stayed in contact with Lee Malvo, and he has noticed drastic changes in the youth since his separation from Muhammad. "He has really turned from being a scripted, indoctrinated soldier into more of a normal, teenage boy. He has become more juvenile, more adolescent. His facial expressions have changed, his demeanor has changed. Now we have more of a boy on our hands." The childhood Malvo had lost has been found, but it is all too late. He will remain in jail for the rest of his life.

John Muhammad remained silent about his crimes, except for a few rare days at his trial when he chose to defend himself. Police have never been able to prove that Muhammad pulled the trigger in any of the shootings. Consequently, he was prosecuted under what is known as "The Triggerman's Statute," which states that if the subject is a direct helper or causing agent of a crime, he should be held responsible for it. John Muhammad is currently on Death Row in Virginia.

John Muhammad and Lee Malvo have also been forensically linked to murders committed in Alabama, Louisiana, Texas, Washington State and Georgia.

FBI HIGH RISK REGISTER—
JOHN MUHAMMAD AND LEE MALVO:
1. Alcohol abuse
2. Drug abuse
3. Psychiatric history

4. Criminal history
5. Sexual problems
6. Physical abuse
7. Psychological abuse
8/9. Dominant father figure aligned with a negative relationship with male caretaker figures
10. Negative relationships with both natural mother and or adoptive mother
11. Treated unfairly
12. Head trauma
13. Demon seed

John Allen Muhammad

1	2	3	4	5	6	7	8/9	10	11	12	13	%
0	0	0	X	0	0	0	00	0	0	0	0	7.7

Lee Boyd Malvo

1	2	3	4	5	6	7	8/9	10	11	12	13	%
0	0	0	0	0	0	X	00	0	X	X	0	23

CHAPTER 7

DR. HAROLD SHIPMAN

"It is difficult to believe that we were friends with
Shipman, who was one of the biggest serial killers in
Great Britain, but he was such a normal guy, he just
fooled everybody. He shouldn't be playing God...
nobody should be doing that."

Colin Shotbolt, friend of Harold Shipman

IN SEPTEMBER 1998, Harold Shipman was convicted of fifteen murders. Since that date, the Shipman Inquiry that was established to investigate his crimes has documented that he had in fact killed 284 people over a period of thirty years. That figure may rise yet again.

The Shipman case is unusual. There was no highly publicized trail of bodies, no madman on the loose. His crimes only came to light when Shipman was arrested in connection with the death of Kathleen Grundy. If

Kathleen Grundy's daughter Angela Woodruff had not asked questions over her mother's death—and over a suspicious will her mother supposedly drew up leaving a small fortune to Shipman—the doctor's crimes may never have come to light, and his murderous career could have carried on.

Angela Woodruff was naturally distraught when she learned of her mother's death, but her distress was not in any way assuaged when she met with her mother's general practitioner, Dr. Harold Shipman. Angela was concerned that her mother had died so suddenly. Although she was eighty-two years old, Kathleen Grundy had been a healthy, lively woman. When Angela asked for an autopsy to be performed on her mother to investigate the cause of death, Shipman did his best to talk her out of it. He assured Angela that he had been with her mother shortly before she died and had since pronounced her dead himself. There was nothing unusual in her death, he assured Angela.

The more she thought about her mother's death, the more suspicious Angela became. She went back and considered the facts of her mother's death. Kathleen Grundy was an active member of her community, and when she did not arrive at the local Age Concern Club where she worked as a volunteer meal server her absence was noted immediately. Kathleen was a former mayor, an affluent and tireless member of her community. Her routine was as regular as clockwork and punctuality and efficiency were her hallmarks. It was unusual for her not to turn up for an appointment without informing anyone. Friends went to her residence, where they found her lying dead on her sofa.

The person they called on to certify her death was another equally respected member of the community, Dr. Harold Shipman. When Shipman arrived, he claimed to have attended Kathleen just a few hours beforehand. He told her friends that he had wanted to extract some samples of her blood as part of a study he was conducting into aging. Shipman quickly pronounced Mrs. Grundy dead. At this point, things seemed to be going his way. It was only when Angela Woodruff arrived and asked for an autopsy that the first cracks began to appear in the Shipman edifice of murder.

The seeds of doubt planted in her mind, Angela Woodruff's suspicions regarding Shipman were exacerbated following a phone call she received from a solicitor who claimed to be holding a copy of her mother's will. She was informed that her mother had recently amended her will in favor of Dr. Shipman, leaving him about $500,000. Angela was astonished. Not only was she a solicitor herself, but she worked for the firm that held her mother's original will, drawn up twelve years previously.

Angela demanded to see the document, and when she did she immediately recognized it for the forgery that it was. There was no way that her precise, studious mother, could have been responsible for such a poorly typed and worded document. As forgeries went, it was one of the worst she had seen.

At first, Angela refused to believe that Shipman himself had forged the will, thinking that someone was trying to frame him. But she could see no reason why this should be so. Eventually, after making her own inquiries and talking with people involved in handling the will,

Angela was forced to come to the unpalatable conclusion that Dr. Shipman had not only forged the will, but that he had murdered her mother, too.

The police were now invited to take a look at Mrs. Grundy's "new" will. It did not take them long to decide it was time to arrest Dr. Harold Shipman and request an autopsy to be performed on the now-buried Kathleen Grundy. For this Detective Superintendent Bernard Postles, heading the investigation, would require an exhumation order from the coroner. Orders such as these are hard to obtain, but in this case the order was granted. It was not the last exhumation order to be issued as the case against Shipman developed. When Chief Coroner Dr. John Pollard examined the body, he found that "there were levels of Diamorphine in the body of the deceased that were sufficient to lead to her death. Of course, Mrs. Grundy had not been suffering any serious illnesses that required the administration of Diamorphine. At that stage, I was totally convinced here that we had someone who had committed many heinous crimes." Whatever is done in the darkness, eventually must come to light. In Shipman's case, the light came as a direct result of his deluded fantasy that he could never be caught.

When the body of Kathleen Grundy was examined, it was quickly established that the high morphine content found in her body had, without question, caused her death and that this would have occurred within a few hours of her receiving the overdose.

There was no doubt in the investigating detectives' minds that this catastrophic misuse of the drug had not been of Mrs. Grundy's own doing, as Shipman told them in one of his later typically defamatory stories. He would calmly go on to claim that the elderly ex-mayor was a helpless drug addict, totally dependent on her next fix of morphine. According to Bernand Postles, Detective Superintendent with Greater Manchester Police, "When they searched Shipman's home, they found the will and the fact of the matter was that his fingerprints were found on it, when he denied ever seeing it. Shipman owned the typewriter the will had been typed on, and during an interview, he suggested that Mrs. Grundy used to borrow the typewriter. But he couldn't suggest to us who returned the machine to him after she borrowed it." In addition to the incriminating typewriter, police searching Shipman's home also found many other incriminating documents such as the medical records of deceased patients.

Shipman, it was learned, had also backdated Mrs. Grundy's medical records. This gave the impression that she was addicted to drugs, specifically Diamorphine.

"The thought of an elderly former lady mayoress of the town of Hyde scoring bags of drugs in the back streets of Manchester seems to me ludicrous and ridiculous, and a gross insult to her memory," says Dr. John Pollard.

In addition, Shipman was also found to have a large amount of jewelery hidden in his garage. This begged the question: To whom did it belong? Just as unusual, Shipman's house was also found to be in an extremely untidy condition. Stacks of old, decaying newspapers littered the floors, as did piles of dirty clothing and unwashed dishes. This was not the sort of domestic arrangement to be expected of a respected pillar of the community.

From a psychological perspective, this seemed to reflect the defiant inner struggle of an outwardly ordered and sanitary individual, and was further evidence of the many paradoxes in the life of Harold Shipman. When it later became known that, in addition to being a liar and a grossly ineffectual document forger, this short, bespectacled and well-thought of doctor was, in fact, a killer many times over, his friends and patients found it hard to accept. Inevitably, the questions arose: Why did this man do it and where did he come from? What made him a monster?

In order to find out whether Harold Shipman was born to kill, we need to examine his early childhood, looking for patterns of behavior to indicate that he carried traits and that his temperament was different.

"With Harold, we find that on the surface he seemed like a very ordinary child, with an ordinary childhood, but if we look deeper, we may find clues why he ended up where he did," says Dr. David Holmes.

Harold Frederick Shipman was born on Friday, June 14, 1946, into a working class home on a council housing estate in Nottingham. It was an estate which, despite being populated by many decent, hardworking families, had acquired the unsavory reputation of being likened to the Wild West, due to the rise in local domestic disturbances.

From the beginning, the baby was referred to as Fred or Freddy and his mother, Vera, wasted little time in instilling within her new son the same superior views that she herself held dear. Vera was the illegitimate daughter of a lace clipper, and perhaps the stigma of being born out of wedlock affected her own self-image, leading to an almost compulsive need to bring her own children up "prim and proper."

Vera's plans for little Fred were grand ones indeed. To her delight, he proved to be a quick learner. Vera was immensely satisfied with how her young boy was turning out. He patterned her philosophies and mirrored her opinions—especially the idea that he was somehow better than the neighbors. In this regard, Fred would go on to surpass his mother's lofty sense of superiority.

He was Vera's boy, there was no doubt about that. He was her favorite and the most promising of the three Shipman children. Neighbors don't recall Mrs. Shipman as being an unpleasant neighbor, just a little haughty. She was perfectly civil to others, but was not shy in letting them know that she held them in low esteem. "They were a lovely family," recalled one of her neighbors. "[Shipman's parents] wanted the children to be different. They didn't want them to be like other kids on the estate, they wanted something better for them."

As young Fred grew up, he emulated much of his mother's outward behavior. The boy's father, Harold, the son of a hosiery warehouseman, had little impact on the boy's development and was certainly not the overpowering presence in the house that Vera was. Even though Fred missed out on a strong relationship with his father, he did not seem overly concerned by this—he always had his mom.

Since Vera was the one who selected her son's playmates, Fred consequently had problems relating to other children. He was not able to gravitate towards the type of people he would normally befriend. Instead, he had to try to adapt his personality to suit the type of children his mother wanted him to like—whether *he* liked it or not. Fred did his best to get on with the playmates his mother selected for him, but it is safe to say that none of them ever became his friends.

For school, Fred was routinely dressed by his mother and she made sure he always looked as if he were going to church. Indeed, even when not attending Whitemoor Primary, Fred was instructed by his mother to be nicely dressed at all times, frequently sporting a tie. It was Vera's fastidious way of visually expressing her boy's "special" quality. An impeccable uniform to complement his unique talents and abilities. Groomed in every way to be the proper little gentlemen from the outset.

Young Shipman was always a loner. He would wile away many hours studying by himself and trying hard to fulfill his mother's dreams of greatness for him. She had built him into an arrogant young boy, constantly reminding him how special he was and reiterating how all the other boys around him were going nowhere in life and were not worth wasting his time with. Instead of dashing off to play with the other neighborhood children, Fred's life revolved around study and suffocating motherly love. Everything—and everybody—else he seemed to hold in contempt.

Little is known of Shipman's sexual fantasy structure at this time. Any tendencies towards sexual deviance that may have blossomed during his isolation are not known. It would be a fair assumption to speculate that a common adolescent dream of power and control over other people's lives developed at this stage in his life. Eventually, he did of course develop a God-complex and this had to have started somewhere.

All of this isolation, when a child should be mixing with others of a similar age and learning the fundamental social skills necessary for mature development, were for all intents and purposes denied him. Thus, the boy grew into a withdrawn teenager that enjoyed no close relationships beyond that with his mother. He had no idea what it was like to have a real friend.

Once in his teens, Harold Shipman's appearance around that of his more casually dressed peers seemed to have had some adverse effects, in terms of name-calling, bullying or simple mockery directed at his "different" look. Young Fred had to get up before 7:00 a.m. and make the long journey across town to get to school, often lugging around a backpack loaded with books. "Plodder," they called him, as he trudged his way back and forth to school carrying his heavy load.

It was often dark when Fred arrived home, and he would open up his workbooks right away and begin to study. He would spend the rest of his evening poring over his academic texts and various other reading matter. He was a voracious studier who felt safer and more secure with his books than he did with people.

Shipman appears to have displayed no outward resistance towards Vera's control of his behavior, dress and life goals. How the pubescent boy dealt with all this internally is another matter entirely. One can imagine how Fred must have felt at times, so removed from the lifestyles of his peers. It is no wonder that Harold Shipman was a somewhat lonely and withdrawn boy, only really close to his domineering mother. He was aware of the fact that he was very much the apple of his doting matriarch's eye and that *in* her eyes he could do no wrong. She had bred in him an ability to form a general disdain for most of those around him. It was something he could never shake off and it was this sense of superiority that would remain with him until the end of his days.

When he finished primary school, it looked as though all Fred's hard work had paid off because he won a place at High Pavement Grammar School, Nottingham's finest seat of learning. For the working-class boy and his pushy mother, it was a big step up. "Fred was very serious, and I think it may be that he had to work harder than most. I know he had a real respect for his family. I think he thought that his parents had made an effort, a real sacrifice. Because he seemed more mature... so much older, for instance, when certain instances took place at school, which had it happened to anyone else, you would have had a good laugh and made them pay for it, with Fred you didn't. People just respected him, and it was strange," recalls Mike Heath, a former school friend. "The school appreciated people like Fred," remembers his classmate Bob Studholme. "He came in and got attention, caused no problems and became a doctor. Feet in working class, head in middle class." As neat and accurate an assessment as this may be, Shipman's path to success was not so straightforward.

Around the age of fifteen, life began to get difficult for Shipman. Despite the hours of lonely study he put in, he found that his grades began to fall. Perhaps even worse than dropping to the bottom of the class, Shipman found himself among the "average" boys—not a shining star nor a struggler that needed help. Suddenly, he was mediocre, nothing special, ordinary. How could *he*, Freddy Shipman, not be top of the class? His over-confidence took a severe dent that not even his mother could restore.

When we ask ourselves what was happening to Fred the answers, as ever, are complex. It is extremely likely that a wealth of frustrations and negative forces had been building within his fragile mental sphere, especially at such an emotionally tumultuous stage in his young life. Physically maturing but emotionally a mommy's boy, he was trapped between two states of being, confused and insecure about who he was, especially now that his poor performance at school had shown him that he was not invincible. And neither was his mother. Fred's already shaky self-belief was shattered when he discovered that his mother had contracted terminal lung cancer.

This was the woman who had influenced every area of her son's developing life, and now her dying days were to influence the rest of his entire life. In the short term, Fred became his mother's full-time caretaker, tending to her every need. Unable to concentrate on his studies, he would sit lost in grim contemplation of his mother's condition. He was painfully aware that she would soon be leaving him forever. She had done her best to prepare him for the world, but she had not done it in a particularly healthy way. She had filled him to the brim with self-confidence but, as Freddy had already begun to appreciate, he was not the child prodigy she had so desperately craved. How could he possibly continue to live up to the role that had been created for him once his mother had gone?

Vera Shipman died in 1963, when Fred was just seventeen. He grieved for his mother in a very isolated and private way. He made barely any reference to her death to his school friends. At night, whatever the weather was like, he would run for miles, dressed only in running shorts and a T-shirt. Mick Heath, who was friendly with Shipman at the time, recalled that "after she died he went to school as if nothing had happened. I found out by accident. I asked him what he had done the night before and he said, 'Oh, my mom died.' He said he had gone for a run. He ran for miles, 'til two or three in the morning. I remembered it had been a terrible night, pelting with rain." Unable to share his grief with anyone, Fred instead was living in his own private hell. The bubble of self-security that his mother had created for Fred was about to burst. With Vera gone, who would tell him how great he was, who would sing his praises? He realized that he would have to do it himself, but was he worth it? His inner torment must have been immense.

His mother dead and his schoolwork suffering, it seems that it was around this time that Harold Shipman formed a deliberate intention to begin assuming control of those around him. In her feeble dying state, he had started with his mother. By taking complete control of her care, he had made her totally dependent on him. One consequence of this was that Fred was able to monitor the administration of doses of pain-killing morphine to his dying mother. For the first time in his life, he held the power of life and death in his hands—and over no less a person than his own mother.

The sense of power this situation gave to Fred was huge. So potent was his desire to repeat such an intense feeling, he knew he would be unable to resist. This would be his calling, the thing that would drive him in the future and compensate for his, by now obvious, inadequacies. But how would he be able to do this? He needed a plan. He needed to be in a position where he had ready access to drugs. It was decided—he would become a doctor.

For many other people with extremely low self-esteem who go on to become serial killers, having a goal and achieving it are often very far apart. Kenneth Bianchi, "The Hillside Strangler," always wanted to be a policeman, for example, but never made it. This was almost the case with Harold Shipman. He took his A-Levels and failed them abysmally. However, displaying the dogged, single-minded character trait for which he was known, Harold eventually secured the grades he needed and won a place at Leeds University Medical School. This was two years after his mother died.

At the university, Shipman had to learn how to mix socially with other people. He was away from home, on his own and needed to adapt. He developed a superficial charm as a self-preservation mechanism, but could never truly feel relaxed with those around him. Inside he watched with amusement as his peers, in his opinion, acted like buffoons. In reality, they were merely acting their age and indulging in the usual sort of pranks associated with students. All except Fred. Just like when he was a boy, Fred once again began to look down on his contemporaries as his inferiors. His old sense of superiority, severely dented by his hard time in grammar school and his mother's death, began to reassert itself.

Shipman's fellow medical students remember little of him from these years. He is described by some of them as "quiet" and "unremarkable," but beyond that few people have anything to say about him. However, he was not at this time entirely the passive loner we may think of him as. One year after beginning his degree, twenty-year-old Harold Shipman met, courted and impregnated seventeen-year-old Primrose Oxtoby. She was not a particularly attractive young lady, though Fred was quite taken with her. The imminent arrival of their first baby was all the invitation he needed to propose to the girl, and they were duly married. Interestingly, there is not a single existing photograph of the couple on their wedding day. This seems somehow symbolic of the mirage of normalcy that was Harold Shipman's life.

With his medical studies and his marriage, Fred was learning how to be *seen* as a good person. During this time he would develop the social skills that would help him create the façade that would allow him to become a well-regarded person in his community. In 1974, Shipman graduated and went on to Pontefract General Infirmary to train as a junior doctor. According to the Shipman Enquiry, this is where Fred committed his first murder. In the words of Mikaela Sitford, journalist and author of the Shipman book *Addicted to Murder*, "The Inquiry found that he killed a four-year-old girl. She was very, very ill and dying, and her mother left the room, saying, 'Please be kind to her,' and he took that as his cue to kill her... he might have pretended that that was euthanasia, that he was doing that child a favor. But [think of] that child in her mother's arms. Her mother was having a cup of tea in the hospital café. So even then, I think he had a very cruel streak that wanted to end lives, come what may."

Psychologist Dr. David Holmes agrees that Shipman's time at Pontefract General Infirmary may have kickstarted his killing career. "It is absolutely uncertain exactly where Harold Shipman began to kill people. It may have been the case of the four-year-old girl. But we do know, as he approached that time, Harold would have had some swelling, some strangely inexplicable, pleasurable feelings that were probably associated with the events with his mother, and he would suddenly begin to feel he was in that powerful role, that controller of life and death, that harks back to that very moment when he thought that he should have been that general practitioner by his mother's bedside." Twelve months after entering Pontefract General Infirmary, Shipman finished his medical training and took a job in general practice.

The Abraham Ormerod Medical Center is in Todmorden, a small town in West Yorkshire, England. When Shipman joined the practice, all seemed well on the surface with the young doctor. However, there is strong evidence to suggest that he was at the time addicted to Pethidine, a painkiller from the *opioid analgesics* group of medicines. He was also forging his patients' medical records and prescriptions on a regular basis. This was not known at first and, as far as everyone was concerned, Shipman was a good doctor.

"Harold was extremely good," says Dr. Michael Grieve, senior general practitioner at Todmorden. "He carried out his duties and brought us all the latest techniques, and kept us very much up to the mark. At the time, he was very much an answer to a prayer... he was just what we needed. The doctors did not choose their patients. The patients chose the doctor that they liked, and Fred had quite a devoted following who felt he was the bees' knees, and would do the best for them in all circumstances."

But it was not long before Dr. Shipman's colleagues noticed a negative side to their workmate. Dr. Grieve recalls, "Fred wouldn't delegate... he wouldn't let the nurses give injections for him, for instance. He wouldn't let the pathology technicians, when they came out once a week, take blood samples from patients. Now Fred was doing all these himself."

Further problems surfaced when the young doctor, not yet thirty, began having blackouts. Showing a talent for deception and resourcefulness, Fred put his blackouts down to a form of epilepsy. But the darker truth soon emerged when the receptionist at Todmorden discovered some unusual entries in a druggist's controlled narcotics ledger, written in Dr. Fred's handwriting. There it was in black and white, laid out in Shipman's own methodical hand, how he had been regularly prescribing large quantities of Pethidine. In his deception, the doctor had even used the names of several of his patients as recipients of the drug. In addition, she noted how Shipman had also recorded orders, using the address of Todmorden medical practice for numerous Pethidine prescriptions. The volume of these orders was excessive to say the least, and Fred Shipman was called to account.

Amid hot denials and pleas for leniency from his colleagues, Fred fought for his career. But as the evidence against him mounted, Fred reacted with uncharacteristic fury. Instead of arguing his case, the cornered Shipman reacted like the petulant child he always was—and always would be. He aimed a vicious kick at the medical bag at his feet, and his colleagues looked on in astonishment as the bag flew across the room and Fred Shipman stormed out of the office.

Chastened and thoroughly caught, with no mother around to tell him it was going to be OK, Shipman was unable to control himself. He had been humiliated in front of his peers—the very people he looked down on. It must have been a truly demoralizing experience for the arrogant young doctor. Until a final decision was made on what to do with him, Fred was forced to live in limbo. "He became manic in all that he did," remembers Dr. Grieve. "He thought that I was the devil incarnate. I never spoke to him again."

Eventually, a decision was made and in 1975 Shipman was forced out of the practice and struck off from the West Yorkshire medical register. He retreated to a drug rehabilitation center to lick his wounds, vowing to return to medicine. Two years later, following an almost $1,000 fine for prescription and drug forgery offenses, Shipman found employment at a new medical practice—in Hyde.

The Donnybrook Surgery in Hyde, Manchester, was at the heart of a close-knit community. According to

Mikaela Sitford, "Hyde was such a traditional town. An old-fashioned community where sons and daughters still lived on their parents' doorsteps. They all knew each other and all trusted one another. So for Shipman to kill so many people was doubly devastating." Colin Shotbolt, a local businessman and former patient of Shipman's, agrees. "Hyde is not a very big town, and my late wife and I knew a great many of Fred's patients. Everyone had the same opinion—that he was a caring guy. You know, he was a normal guy. We went to a couple of social functions with [the Shipmans]. They were good company outside, and extremely popular with everybody who was there... giving the impression that the guy was just a normal guy. Most times he was okay. Sometimes he was a bit offish, you know. What were those days? Maybe those were the days something happened...you just don't know...it makes you think."

Reprising his outwardly respectable, tweed-wearing image as a diligent and compassionate local doctor, Shipman fit easily into life as a Hyde general practitioner. All the while, however, he was masking his natural condescending attitude towards his fellow man. Despite the occasional revealing burst of sarcasm aimed at the odd, recalcitrant visitor to his office, Shipman focused completely on gaining his patients' absolute trust and earning his colleagues' respect. In this, he succeeded.

The simmering cauldron that was Harold "Fred" Shipman, a man who had never forgotten the indignities he had suffered as a result of his own lies and weaknesses, was now back in a position of power and trust. In the years to come, as he repeatedly and casually stole the lives from so many of the town's elderly residents, he was hailed as "the most marvelous doctor in Hyde."

He was now firmly in control of his own destiny—and of the destiny of the many others who had placed their lives in the good doctor's hands. The elderly and the sick of Hyde could not possibly have known of their significance to Harold Shipman—that they were unwitting lambs for slaughter by the likeable new doctor.

It is not known exactly how far back in time we must travel to locate Harold Shipman's first victim, or indeed to determine decisively the final number of those who fell prey to him. What we do know is exactly how Shipman went about his callous task of murder. Recreating the "care" he gave to his dying mother, Shipman would inject his victims with lethal doses of morphine and then watch them as they slowly lost consciousness and died. This usually took place in the victims' homes. Chief Coroner John Pollard notes:

The way in which many of the victims were found was, in itself, quite disturbing. Many of them were found fully clothed in the middle of the daytime...often sitting upright in a chair, or on a sofa. In some of those cases, Shipman had certified on the cremation form that he had carried out a full external examination of the body, yet the victim was still sitting there, fully clothed... shoes on, sleeves buttoned down to the wrists, dresses buttoned up to the neck. Well, how you can carry out a full external examination under those circumstances, I just don't understand.

For more than twenty-three years, this man snatched away life after life. He was his victims' Grim Reaper, cloaked in the guise of somebody who cared. Each victim added to his sense of invincibility. The more he killed, the more powerful he became. His twisted reasoning told him: If you can be stopped, why didn't they stop you? The very fact that he could dispatch person after person, with nobody noticing what he was doing, only served to enhance the message in his brain: You are God and you cannot be stopped.

This is the grandest of all grand delusions, and it would be the one that would ultimately bring Shipman down. In fact, it is the element that brings down most multiple killers—their overwhelming sense of their own superiority. Their over-confidence breeds contempt, and their dumbfounding arrogance leads inevitably to a climactic mental implosion. Simply speaking, these self-proclaiming messiahs overload. Convinced that they are possessed of a force akin to magic, they eventually become careless. Nothing they do could ever result in their capture and subsequent judgment, they honestly believe. Shipman was a classic example of this. Unfortunately, it just took a lot longer for the signs of Shipman's megalomania to be uncovered.

In terms of sexual deviance, Shipman does not fit the classic sexual serial killer mold. The majority of such murderers will have some form of direct sexual contact with their victims. Along with Shipman, an exception is New York's infamous "Son Of Sam" killer, David Berkowitz. Although he never sexually assaulted any of his victims before or after shooting them dead, he would

administered to his dying mother. Unlike his mother, most of his victims were old. The majority were over the age of seventy-five.

Harold Shipman is suspected of approximately two hundred and eighty murders. In terms of sheer numbers, this makes him the world's worst serial killer. Some feel that "Doctor Death" may, in fact, be responsible for up to one thousand slayings. Whatever the actual figure, he eclipses the toll of any other serial killer caught to date. Ultimately, he was convicted of the murders of fifteen people. Once imprisoned, like Fred West before him, he saw that his reason for existence had been taken away from him and on January 13, 2004, he hung himself in his cell at H.M. Prison Wakefield, in North Yorkshire, England. He left behind him no testament or single explanation for any of his crimes. It was to be his final act of control, knowing that he would leave behind a world asking "Why?" There would be no answers. A mystery man to the end, Dr. Shipman would not have had it any other way. In a final, bizarre twist to his medical and murderous career, not long before he died Harold Shipman saved the life of fellow inmate Tony Fleming, when he attempted suicide in their prison cell.

In this macabre tale, Dr. Shipman's former patients are grateful that he was finally stopped. There is little doubt that many people today owe their lives to a determined and intelligent woman named Angela Woodruff. If she had not asked questions over her mother's death, who knows how many more lives Shipman would have taken? Ann Alexander, solicitor for families in the Shipman Inquiry, gives this poignant comment on what many of

Shipman's actual victims must have been thinking on the day of their deaths: "Many of his victims regarded [Shipman's house calls] as something to look forward too. There were many instances of them being dressed in their best clothes. They were getting a visitor and it was something they were looking forward to, and therefore, let's put on something nice, because the doctor is coming to visit."

In the end, Shipman made two convicting mistakes that ultimately brought him down. Mistake number one was using morphine on his victims. It is one of the few poisons that can remain in body tissue for centuries. In the words of Chief Coroner John Pollard, "There are other drugs he could have used that would have been less traceable, or not traceable at all, within the body. Why Shipman chose to use Diamorphine, I don't know. One reason might be that he was simply not quite as clever as he thought he was, and didn't realize that it was so traceable so easily. The other reason is, that maybe, I don't know. Maybe... he wanted to be found out at some stage." Mistake number two was the typewriter used to forge Kathleen Grundy's will. Was this some sort of test on Shipman's part? Was he pushing credibility to the limit to see if he really was above suspicion?

Of course we can all speculate over how and why Dr. Shipman turned into a serial killer, and author Christopher Berry-Dee has his own theory. "I think that it is highly plausible to suggest that Harold eventually realized that his mother had literally stolen a healthy childhood from him. She had controlled his every waking moment, even to the degree of selecting friends for him and ordering the boy what to wear, day after day, instilling in him all the while that everyone else was beneath him. The borderline between love and hate can be as narrow as cotton thread, so while he was ministering to her during her final days, perhaps he was loving her and hating her at once? She had controlled him throughout his life and now was cheating him, abandoning him in death. Perhaps so embedded was a hatred for his elderly mother, that maybe for him, it was payback time."

We will leave the final word on this most untypical of serial killers to criminologist and forensic profiler Dr. David Holmes. "The very remarkable thing about Shipman's case is that is he was not remarkable. The kind of people, the elderly people he picked, are what we call the category of 'less than dead.' In other words, the type of people you don't actually notice if they pass away. They are not the kind of people who are going to cause a big fuss. And in fact, counter to most serial killers, he was probably one of the only people to get the relatives, or the council, to take away the bodies for him."

FBI HIGH RISK REGISTER—DR. HAROLD SHIP-MAN:

1. Alcohol abuse
2. Drug abuse
3. Psychiatric history
4. Criminal history
5. Sexual problems
6. Physical abuse

7.   Psychological abuse

8/9.   Dominant father figure aligned with a negative
        relationship with male caretaker figures

10.   Negative relationships with both natural mother
        and or adoptive mother

11.   Treated unfairly

12.   Head trauma

13.   Demon seed

1	2	3	4	5	6	7	8/9	10	11	12	13	%
0	0	0	0	0	0	0	0	0	0	0	0	0

CHAPTER 8

DEAN ARNOLD CORLL: THE CANDY MAN

"Dean Corll decided he wanted to have sex with them. They wouldn't let him, so he killed them, brought them out here and buried them."

Elmer Wayne Henley

WITH HIS TWO accomplices, Dean Corll was a sado-sexual homosexual serial murderer who preyed on the boys of Houston. He gained their trust, lured them to his home, and raped and murdered them. The victims were hitchhikers or vagrants that one of his accomplices would find for him. They were taken to Corll's house, where they would be wined and dined until they passed out from being drunk or they were drugged. The victims were then strapped or handcuffed to Corll's torture board. They would then be sodomized and tortured, sometimes for

days. He would pull out their pubic hairs one by one, insert glass rods into their penises and place large, bullet-like items in their rectums. Most of the bodies were buried under a boathouse that Corll was renting, while other bodies were buried on a nearby island and in a lake.

Dean Corll was born on Christmas Eve 1939, in Fort Wayne, Indiana, the first child of Arnold and Mary Corll. While Mary adored her oldest son, her husband—a factory worker who became an electrician—found children tire-some. Mary and Arnold were temperamentally unsuited and divorced when Dean was six years old.

Despite later attempts at reconciliation, including remarrying, Mrs. Corll was left alone to support Dean and his younger brother, Stanley. They were left in the care of an elderly couple while their mother went out to work.

Like so many emerging serial killers, from the very beginning Dean was an over-sensitive loner. Because his feelings had been hurt at a birthday party when he was six years old, he refused to go to other people's houses. In 1950, it was discovered that he had a congenital heart ailment and he was ordered to avoid all school sports. Thereafter, he took up the trombone, and a classmate recalled, "He was a very good musician and a nice guy." The family was now living in Houston, and life for Mrs. Corll was hard, working while the boys went to one school after another.

Already, we can start to tick off boxes in the FBI's High Risk Register: unhappy parents, loss of the patriarch, mother largely absent, disruptive education, and sickly.

In 1953, Mary Corll married a traveling clock salesman named Jake West, by whom she had a daughter. They moved to Vidor, Texas, a small town where, as one com-

mentator put it, "the biggest event for the kids was to pour kerosene on the cat and set it afire."

With both parents largely absent, Dean became a kind of surrogate father to his younger siblings. One day, a pecan nut salesman observed Mrs. West's efficiency at baking pies and asked her why she didn't take up candy making. She liked the idea, and was soon running a candy business from their garage, with Jake West as the traveling salesman and Dean as the errand boy. Though often overworked, Dean was cheerful and uncomplaining.

After graduating from high school at the age of twenty, Dean returned to Indiana to be with Jake West's widowed mother while his family returned to Houston and continued with the candy business. Two years later, Dean moved back to Houston and took a job with the Houston Lighting and Power Company. He worked at the candy factory at night, impressing co-workers with his industry.

In 1964, Dean Corll was drafted into the army. This was a watershed in his life, and it was when he first realized that he might be a homosexual. Released from the army after eleven months—pleading that his family needed him to work in the candy business—he returned to Houston to find his mother's second marriage in trouble. Mr. and Mrs. West had become business rivals rather than partners, and when Jake West threw her out of the shop one day, Mary went off and opened one of her own at West 22nd Street near Helms Elementary School in the Heights area of Houston.

Dean found an apartment of his own and began making friends with the neighboring children—notably the boys—by giving away free candy. Yet, when a boy who worked for the company made some kind of sexual advance towards Dean, he became upset and his mother, who remained intensely protective of her son, dismissed the errand boy. Dean, it seems, had not accepted his homosexuality at this point.

Mary got married again, this time to a merchant seaman. The marriage soon ran into trouble. She even suspected that her new husband might have been having an affair. Following the pattern of her previous marriage, they divorced and then remarried. Despite this, Jake West's jealousy of his second-time-around wife's happiness forced them to separate again. His threats also destroyed her enthusiasm for the candy business. When a psychic told her to move to Dallas, she took his advice. Divorcing yet again, she closed the candy factory and moved there in 1968.

Dean, now left alone in Houston, took a job as an electrician. Suddenly free to do as he liked, in 1970 he renewed his acquaintance with a former friend, fifteen-year-old David Brooks, and a strange partnership began.

Wednesday, August 8, 1973, was a typically hot Texan summer's day. At 8:00 a.m. the temperature had already climbed to 130 degrees. It was the sort of blistering morning when no one, man or beast, had energy. The longhorns were listless and the fire ants stayed deep in their nests. Even the asphalt on the roads began to buckle and melt.

But on hot days like this, asphalt isn't the only thing that goes into meltdown. When temperatures rise, so do tempers and the emergency services typically steel themselves for an increase in calls. One 911 emergency call that morning came into the Pasadena Police Department. An excited and agitated voice told the operator, "Y'all better come on here now. I just killed a man."

Two squad cars, with their strobes flashing, screeched into the pleasant, southeastern Houston suburb minutes later looking for 2020 Lamar Drive. This quiet, middle-class section of town featured a number of attractive-looking homes, and the police stopped outside one of them—a green and white small-frame bungalow. Outwardly, it was neat and tidy except for a tired tree and a slightly overgrown lawn.

The officers climbed out of their dusty cruisers, and one wiped the toe of his high boot on his grey uniform pants, noting hot oil dripping from the V8's sump onto the ground. The cops' attentions were first drawn to two boys and a half-dressed girl huddled together on the front doorstep of the property. The three teenagers were distraught and had been crying; the girl was rocking back and forth in a state of shock, with the boys half-heartedly attempting to console her while at the same time wrestling with their own anxieties.

Their hands cautiously lingering close to their revolvers, the police looked at each other, nodded in the affirmative and then approached. One of the youths, a thin, gangly boy, peered up at them. By all accounts he was very striking, although his cheeks were marred with acne and his upper lip bore the wispy blonde beginnings of an immature moustache. He contemplated the two patrolmen with tearful, red-rimmed blue eyes, and in a thick Texan drawl, he informed the officers that he had summoned their assistance.

When patrolman A.B. Jamison asked where the body was, the youth slowly turned and pointed through the open front door, saying, "He's in there." In the hallway, slumped against a wall, Jamison saw the bullet-ridden body of a white male. It was Dean Corll—6 feet tall, 200 pounds, with dark hair greying at the temples, his face now a bloody mask. The cop called for backup, and homicide officers were soon on their way. The medical examiner would recover six bullets from the body, one of which was lodged in Corll's head. They didn't know it at the time, but Corll's violent demise brought to an end an era of almost unimaginable horror.

The 911 caller was seventeen-year-old Elmer Wayne Henley. In a shaking voice, the skinny youth explained to the officers that Dean Arnold Corll had been his friend, and that he had been forced to shoot Dean dead. Henley went on to claim that Corll, a homosexual, had planned to murder him and the other two teenagers, Timothy Kerley and Rhonda Williams. After a short discussion, the three youths were driven to the Pasadena police headquarters, and Dean Corll was taken to the morgue.

Once the ambulance bearing Corll's body had departed the scene, it was time to search the dead man's home. It quickly became apparent to the police that it had only been occupied recently. The few furnishings were sparse and functional and what appeared to be Corll's bedroom, which lay beyond the blood-splattered hallway, consisted of a bed, a small table and little else. A large, surreal-looking poster bearing a Jesus Christ clone image and proclaiming the word "LOVE" in bold lettering hung on a wall.

Detectives noted that the bedroom carpet was covered with a layer of transparent plastic sheeting. An ominous sign. They saw a military-style gas mask resting on the unmade bed. There was also a scarred length of plywood, into which holes had been drilled at each end. Two looped lengths of nylon rope had been threaded through the holes. A set of handcuffs was also attached to this sinister contraption. Amid this grim, sado-masochistic and fetish paraphernalia, a vacuum cleaner was plugged into a wall socket.

Also found by police was a large hunting knife and sheath, a box containing a 17-inch double-headed dildo, several glass tubes and a jar of Vaseline. It seemed at first glance as though Mr. Corll had been something of a sexual deviant, and this was confirmed throughout the bungalow's drab and seedy interior as officers discovered further evidence of the late owner's bizarre sexual preferences.

Parked in the driveway was Corll's 1972 Ford Econoline van. A cursory look inside revealed hooks, rings bolted to the sides of the vehicle, a box large enough to accommodate a folded human body (strands of hair were found inside the box) and coils of rope on the floor. Turning their attention to a shed at the rear of the premises, officers found a similar sized box with air holes drilled in its sides. It didn't take a lot of police imagination to figure out that the deceased man had been using restraints during his sexual activities.

Meanwhile, back at police headquarters, Wayne Henley was explaining to a hushed room of police officers how he had come to shoot his so-called friend, Dean. He began by saying that he and Timothy Cordell Kerley had been invited to Corll's home the previous evening for a paint-sniffing session, or a "huffing" party, as Henley referred to it. Later that night, he said that he and Kerley left Corll's, on the promise that they would come back later. When they returned, they were accompanied by Rhonda Williams, a mutual friend.

Henley went on to tell the officers that Corll took one look at Rhonda Williams and became instantly enraged. Dean Corll didn't like girls; he preferred young boys. He yelled at Wayne, saying he had spoiled everything by bringing a female into their company. After some bickering, however, Henley said Corll seemed to calm down and gave the appearance of being happy, even comfortable with the situation. There were no hard feelings, Corll told his young guests, while apologizing for his overreaction.

The police then learned from Henley that several tins of acrylic paint were cracked open as the quartet began their "huffing" session. After spraying the inside of a paper bag and inhaling the fumes too many times, the three youths became so intoxicated with the noxious fumes that they slowly lost consciousness. Within a short time, they were all laid out on the floor. This was just the way Corll wanted them.

When Henley came to his senses, he was to find the powerfully built Corll looming over him. All traces of his earlier good humor had evaporated. "My ankles were bound," he told the police, "and Corll was snapping handcuffs on my wrists." Looking across the living room, Henley said that he saw his two friends had been similarly bound with ropes and handcuffs. Timothy Kerley had been stripped naked and Rhonda was gagged with a strip of adhesive tape. Henley told the police that Corll was brandishing a knife at them, saying that they were all going to be killed. "But first I'm gonna have my fun," Corll told him.

Desperate to save his life, Henley thought fast and struck a deal with Corll. In return for his release from the cuffs, Henley told Corll that he would rape Rhonda while Corll had his fun with Kerley. Corll agreed, and carried the two still unconscious teenagers into the bedroom. Corll, Henley claimed, rolled Kerley onto his stomach, saying, "You take the girl and I'll mess with Tim."

Handing Henley his hunting knife, Corll ordered the youth to cut off the girl's clothing and assault her. Henley, initially acquiescent, with a view to saving his own skin, finally cracked as Corll began to mount the semi-conscious Kerley. "Why don't you let me take her outta here, Dean? She don't want to see that," Henley yelled over the radio music that Corll had blasted up to full volume to drown out any screams.

Locked into the evident ecstasy of sodomizing Timothy Kerley, Corll did not even acknowledge Henley. At this point, Henley claimed that he picked up Corll's gun and turned it on the man himself. Turning from the bound youth beneath him, Corll challenged Henley to go ahead and shoot, aggressively ridiculing him that he didn't have the guts to do it. Henley moved into the hallway, warning Corll to back away. Corll, with no intention of backing off, charged at Henley who fired a single shot into Corll's face. As the dying Corll slid down the wall, Henley fired off five more rounds, pumping bullets into the man's chest, back and shoulders, before dropping the weapon and rushing to the assistance of his tied-up friends.

In providing a little background to the shooting, Henley told his police questioners that he and Dean had known each other since they had both lived in a comparably low-income area of Houston known as the Heights. Corll was sixteen years older than Henley, and he had assumed a kind of big brother role towards the younger Henley. They had become good enough friends for Henley to have continued his association with Corll when the older man moved into his father's previous property at 2020 Lamar Drive. Corll and Henley hung out together, getting drunk or high, and Henley explained that Dean had been a pretty cool guy until the previous evening.

While detectives were questioning Henley, Timothy Kerley was having his say, too. He told his interrogators, "While we were waiting for the police, Wayne told me that if I wasn't his friend he could have got $1500 for me." Despite his eager assistance, investigators began to ask themselves if there wasn't more to Elmer Wayne Henley than met the eye.

When questioned about the sexual devices discovered at Corll's bungalow, Henley confessed that Corll liked "little boys." Indeed, he went further by admitting to procuring boys for his friend in return for healthy cash payments. When the police asked Henley why things had soured to the point where he had shot his friend, Henley replied, "[Corll] made one mistake. He told me that I wouldn't be the first one he'd killed. He said he'd already killed a lot of boys and buried them in a boatshed."

As Houston police records show, young boys had been disappearing from the Heights area at an alarming rate over the previous three years. Mindful of Henley's almost throw-away comment, the police decided to dig a little deeper. Was Corll in any way connected to these missing boys?

Later that day Henley led police, accompanied by a number of prison custody trustees, to a marina and to the Southwest Boat Storage yard, located at Silver Bell Street, Pasadena. They were looking for Stall Eleven, a corrugated iron shed rented by Dean Corll. Once they located and opened the shed, the officers were unprepared for what they found inside. The first thing that hit them on that scorching day was the unmistakable smell of decaying human flesh. Nothing adverse was obviously visible, though. There was a partially dismantled car, a child's bicycle, a large iron drum, some boxes, two sacks of lime and a plastic bag full of male clothing. The floor was covered by strips of old carpet.

Throwing open the doors to allow fresh air and light into the building, the investigators began to dig. They thought they might find one or two bodies under the floor, but there were much more than that. Just 6 inches below the sandy earth, the first evidence presented itself in the form of a decaying face, with the eye sockets of a boy staring up at the diggers.

The stench was suddenly overpowering—it clenched the mens' throats and assaulted their nostrils. The team gagged and retched as they dug into Corll's private cemetery. One by one, the bodies were recovered from the mass grave. As more human remains were hauled from this hellish charnel house, it became evident that the majority of them were in an advanced state of decomposition. The bodies had been methodically wrapped in plastic. One corpse had been interred sitting upright, two others in the fetal position and another lay on its back, mouth agape as though in a deep slumber. Many limbs were skeletal and scattered in the grave. All of these once living, breathing youths had been reduced to a disintegrating jumble of putrefied flesh and bones.

Adding to the sheer horror of it all was evidence of extreme sexual mutilation. A small plastic bag lay alongside one body, and sealed inside was a perfectly preserved severed penis and testicles. Another boy's penis had been gnawed almost in half, by human teeth it would later be learned. Nearly all of the victims had been gagged, their corpses still bearing evidence of their restraints: Thick twine or Venetian blind cords were bound around most of the victims' necks. Several of the boys had been shot multiple times. Another youth had been kicked to death; his entire chest region had been stamped upon and caved in.

These sickening, perverse injuries were quite clearly the work of a monster, a rabid animal that had abused and annihilated with wanton abandon again and again.

Following this gruesome set of findings, Henley then led investigators to the shores of Lake Sam Rayburn and the beach at High Island. There were more bodies buried in these locations, he claimed. And he was right. An additional eight corpses were recovered from Lake Sam

Rayburn, and six more were dug up from beneath the sand at High Island. Two more bodies that Henley insisted lay buried on the beach were never found, yet this brought the total number of slayings for which Dean Arnold Corll was responsible to twenty-seven.

Thus, in 1973, Dean Corll became the most prolific serial murderer in U.S. history to that date, having taken the homicidal crown from Juan Corona, who had murdered twenty-five itinerant farm workers in California two years previously. Corll's horrifying tally would itself later be eclipsed when John Wayne Gacy hit the headlines in 1978 and the world learned that he had killed at least thirty-three young men and boys, burying most of them in the crawl space beneath his Chicago home.

When asked why Corll had done it, Henley's answer was pathetically simple. "Dean Corll decided he wanted to have sex with them. They wouldn't let him, so he killed them, brought them out here and buried them."

This was clearly a grisly case, but so far, it was relatively open-and-shut, if the account of the talkative Henley was to be believed. The waters began to muddy when another young man called David Brooks came forward. He admitted that he had been present during a number of the Corll slayings, and in fact, had assisted in a number of the burials. Moreover, his account differed in many respects to the one offered by Wayne Henley.

Brooks told police that he had met Corll in 1967. Although he vehemently denied any participation in the murders, Brooks nevertheless painted a stark portrait of seventeen-year-old Henley and the older Corll forging a terrible alliance to indulge their mutually sadistic pursuits.

Henley, it seemed, enjoyed the power the psychopathic Corll bestowed upon him while taking charge of a helpless victim. Indeed, it seems as though Corll delighted in having the young Henley kill alongside him.

Brooks spoke of killings that he had seen at a couple of Corll's previous properties, saying, "It was during the time that we were living on Columbia Street that Wayne Henley got involved. Wayne took part in getting the boys at first, and then later he took an active part in the killings. Wayne seemed to enjoy causing pain and he was especially sadistic at the Schuler address." Recounting one especially brutal episode and searing into the officers' brains just how vicious Henley could be, Brooks said, "There was another boy killed at the Schuler house, actually there were two at this time. A boy named Billy Balch and a Johnny—I think that his last name was Malone. Wayne strangled Billy and he said 'Hey Johnny,' and when Johnny looked up Wayne shot him in the forehead with a .22 automatic. The bullet came out his ear and he raised up and about three minutes later he said, 'Wayne, please don't.' Then Wayne strangled him and Dean helped."

The horrendous torture wreaked upon the helpless victims was heartbreaking. Through the autopsy processes, police discovered that victims had been subjected to the most violent of beatings, whipped and savagely bitten. Large foreign objects had been forced into their rectums and they had all been raped. They had been slowly asphyxiated, given electric shocks and burned with a lighter. Corll had also mercilessly burned their genitals and had forced plastic tubes into his victims' urethras.

Dean Corll's cruelty knew no bounds, but now he was dead, shot six times by his lover and accomplice in sado-sexual homicide. Dean Corll would never face trial. Elmer Wayne Henley, for his part in the slayings, though he always denied actually murdering any of the boys, was sentenced to six consecutive ninety-nine-year life terms, having been convicted of nine counts of first-degree murder. He will never be released. David Brooks, who almost certainly participated in a number of the murders, received just one life term.

Although police recovered a total of twenty-seven bodies, it is likely that Corll murdered many other boys during his years at large as a vicious sex murderer. Henley himself had said that there were at least two more buried on the beach at High Island, and one grave contained an additional bone from an arm and a pelvis, an obvious indicator that another boy, never officially included in the body count, had lain there.

There was also an apparent seven-month hiatus in Corll's murderous diary, which seemed enormously unlikely given his all-consuming passion for homicide. Even police sources acknowledge the high probability that there are other bodies out there that Corll had buried, but as one officer remarked, "What's the point?"

Such cold indifference to the search for other victims was widely criticized in the months and years afterward. However, it was the view of most investigators that they had unearthed more than enough misery. The search for more bodies was discontinued shortly after the last High Island finds.

Dean Corll's craving for ever-increasingly savage violence reigned unchecked. It was obvious that this killer could not be fully satisfied unless he caused maximum pain and suffering to the boys before finally snuffing them out. Obsessed with bondage and sadism, Corll revelled in performing "double" murders, enormously satisfied with the idea of one victim tied up and helpless watching as the other died slowly before him. On a couple of occasions, the victims were brothers. He would have taken extreme pleasure in the knowledge that one pair of brothers whom he slaughtered had a father who was working on a new apartment block next door to the complex in which Corll lived. As the man attended to his project only yards away, the monstrous Corll was raping and torturing his two sons to death.

Corll saw in his young victims everything that he hated about himself. Weakness, vulnerability and disgust at his own perverse advances toward them. His intense sexual attraction to them made him despise them all the more. Growing up in an age when homosexuality itself was seriously frowned upon, Corll's sexual attraction to young boys left him carrying around a heavy burden of internal shame and resentment. Eventually and inevitably, this would boil over and he would degenerate into a sadistic killer, a fury-driven dervish that would destroy as many of these good-looking young boys as he possibly could.

The fact that he was able to draw two others into his nefarious private world is testament to just how truly manipulative this psychopath could be in his efforts to achieve his ghastly goals.

DEAN CORLL'S VICTIMS

Jeffrey Konenm, age eighteen. Murdered:
September 25, 1970

James Glass, age fourteen, and Danny Yates, age fifteen. Murdered: December 15, 1970

Donald Waldrup, age seventeen, and Jerry Waldrup,
age thirteen. Murdered: January 30, 1971

David Hilligiest, age thirteen, and Malley Winkle,
age sixteen. Murdered: May 30, 1971

Ruben Watson, age seventeen. Murdered:
August 17, 1971

Frank Aguirre, age eighteen. Murdered:
February 24, 1972

Billy Baulch, age seventeen, and Johnny Delome,
age sixteen. Murdered: May 21, 1972

Wally Simoneaux, age fourteen, and Richard
Hembree, age thirteen. Murdered: October 3, 1972

Mark Scott, age eighteen. Murdered:
December 22, 1972

Billy Lawrence, age fifteen. Murdered: June 11, 1973

Ray Blackburn, age twenty. Murdered: June 15, 1973

Homer Garcia, age fifteen. Murdered: July 7, 1973

Tony Baulch, age fifteen. Murdered: July 19, 1973

Charles Cobble, age seventeen, and Marty Jones, age
eighteen. Murdered: July 25, 1973

James Dreymala, age thirteen. Murdered:
August 3, 1973

Like two peas from the same pod, there are striking parallels between the homicidal development of Dean Corll
and another serial killer, John Wayne Gacy, whose mur-

der of thirty-three boys stunned Chicago in 1978. Indeed, after he was arrested in Des Plaines, Illinois, Gacy told police that he had carbon-copied Corll's torture board technique because he admired him.

Corll and Gacy were both sons of an indulgent mother and a stern father. Both men had a disability that excluded them from many childhood activities and had heart problems, while Gacy was also epileptic. Corll and Gacy were also dominant personalities with a real capacity to succeed in business. More significantly, both men seemed to have been unaware of their homosexuality until their early twenties. In Corll's case, even after he acknowledged it, he seems to have cherished a dream of one day settling down to a normal married life. John Gacy had the same aspirations.

His father's inability to relate to his sons was a major cause of Dean's emotional withdrawal and repression. Growing boys need a male role model with whom they can identify. The absence of a father figure in his life forced Dean to identify instead with his mother.

Corll and Gacy had one more fundamental resemblance: Both were "Jekyll and Hyde" personalities who were ashamed of their attraction to their own sex. While unable to resist their homosexual impulses, they felt they were failing to be "real" men. At first, Corll's attraction to young boys expressed itself in his role as older brother to his siblings. The "Hyde" persona began to manifest itself when he realized that some boys would indulge in oral sex for money.

Fifteen-year-old David Brooks was one of these boys. Brooks eventually became so emotionally dependant on

Corll that he made no attempt to denounce him when he learned that Corll had murdered two boys. This dependence inevitably contributed to the tragedy that followed, since Brook's willingness to subjugate his will gave free rein to Corll's "Hyde" persona. In time, as oral sex ceased to satisfy him, Corll turned to the sexual violation of his young victims. Brooks admitted, "He killed them because he wanted sex, and they didn't want to."

In conclusion from what we know about the dreadfulness of Corll's crimes and from what we shall soon learn from the tortuous killings carried out by John Gacy, (not to mention other bisexual and homosexual killers such as Randy Kraft), we can see that these types of serial killers subconsciously hated their own sexuality. They were ashamed of what they had become. In torturing and murdering their victims by such agonizing means, they were actually punishing and killing themselves, uprooting and destroying the element within themselves that they so despised.

FBI HIGH RISK REGISTER—DEAN CORLL:

1. Alcohol abuse
2. Drug abuse
3. Psychiatric history
4. Criminal history
5. Sexual problems
6. Physical abuse
7. Psychological abuse
8/9. Dominant father figure aligned with a negative relationship with male caretaker figures

10. Negative relationships with both natural mother and or adoptive mother
11. Treated unfairly
12. Head Trauma
13. Demon seed

1	2	3	4	5	6	7	8/9	10	11	12	13	%
X	X	0	0	X	0	0	XX	0	0	0	?	38.5

CHAPTER 9

JOHN WAYNE GACY: THE KILLING CLOWN

"The dead won't bother you. It's the living you've got to worry about."

John Wayne Gacy on Death Row

JOHN GACY WAS executed by lethal injection at 12:10 a.m. on Tuesday, May 10, 1994, at the Stateville Penitentiary near Joliet, Illinois. Convicted for killing thirty-three young men between 1972 and 1978, he holds the record in America for the largest number of convictions for murder.

John Gacy was a serial killer who was unable to curb his homosexual homicidal perversions. He married twice, but also served a prison sentence in 1968 for committing sodomy. He was a very sexually confused individual. He worked at various times for Kentucky Fried

Chicken, as a shoe salesman and then as a building contractor. In 1971, he moved into a house in Norwood Park, a middle-class suburb of Chicago, which provided a base for both his contracting business and his homicidal activities.

Not unlike Dean Corll, whom Gacy admired, he also plied his prey with drinks and drugs, then used on them what he called his "handcuff trick." This is where he showed his victims how he was able to escape from a pair of handcuffs, and when the victims tried to repeat the trick on themselves they would find themselves trapped and at his mercy. Gacy's thirty-three victims were raped, sodomized and tortured. As with Corll's *modus operandi*, many victims were strapped to Gacy's own version of a torture board. Some were strangled, while others were suffocated to death or stabbed.

Thirty of Gacy's victims were exhumed from the crawl-space beneath his house and the area around his property. Three corpses were found in the Des Plaines River. Only twenty-four of the bodies were identified.

Blue-eyed John Wayne Michael Gacy came into the world at Edgewater Hospital on St. Patrick's Day, March 17, 1942. He was the second of Marion and John Stanley Gacy's three children, and their only son. Joanne was born two years earlier and two years after John, Karen completed the family.

Marion Elaine Gacy, maiden name Robinson, was an outspoken and gregarious woman from Racine, Wisconsin. A vivacious girl, she loved to dance, sing and enjoy a few drinks with her friends. She was also hard-working and had supported herself as a pharmacist prior to her marriage at the age of thirty. Her upbringing had been solid to the core. She was no abusive, hard-drinking butterfly; indeed, our focus is on a thoroughly decent woman.

The family patriarch, John Stanley Gacy, Sr. was born in Chicago, the son of Polish immigrants. Quite the opposite of his wife, he was serious, self-contained, somber and largely incapable of displaying the gentler emotions such as happiness or sorrow. Nevertheless, he was remembered by colleagues as an industrious machinist, a perfectionist in a perfectionist's trade, and he earned a good living.

At home, John Sr. could do anything with his hands: carry out household repairs, decorate, create his own tools—and beat his wife, which he did frequently. Quick-tempered, he could explode without any warning. At dinner, he would lash out at anyone who said so much as a word that displeased him. He also drank heavily, and believed that not whipping the child with a rod was to spoil him.

It would be fair to say that John Jr. had the shakiest of starts in life, since he barely lived through a difficult breech birth. The Gacy's home on Opal Street in Norridge, Chicago, was one of six houses on the street but retained its rural charm. Visitors noticed that prairie grass surrounding the house grew like electric wire in every direction.

Norridge was a small community of like-minded people who cared for their homes and their children. Residents kept livestock, including chickens and goats, and carefully tended their vegetable gardens. Doors were never locked and curtains never twitched with gossip.

Everybody minded their own business and expected their neighbors to mind theirs, too.

Following his near-death birth, John Jr.'s start in life was not without further problems. One day as John Stanley worked on his car, his four-year-old came out to help. However, he messed up a pile of parts that his father had neatly laid out in a specific order. Mr. Gacy liked things orderly. He was expected to deal with tolerances of a thousandth of an inch at work and that, in his view, was the way things should be done at home. His mania for tolerances, however, didn't extend to the treatment he meted out to his family, and little John was no exception. For this slight infraction, Gacy yelled at his son and whipped him with a belt. It was a thrashing John Wayne would remember for the rest of his life.

Around this time, Gacy later claimed that a fifteen-year-old local girl who had minor learning difficulties took John out into the long prairie grass and pulled his pants down. John ran off home and told his mother what had happened. The two families fell out over this incident and bad blood existed between them for years afterwards.

When John Gacy was on Death Row he revived this story as an example of a childhood trauma that contributed to his twisted development. "At the age of three, a fifteen-year-old girl...if you want to call it molesting...she was playing house and I was the baby, and she was playing with my penis; and the parents walked in and broke it up. At age three, what do you know about what she's doing?"

At about five, Johnny began to experience seizures that caused him to pass out for no apparent reason at all. The doctors who examined him did not immediately settle on a precise diagnosis; nevertheless, advising caution, they prescribed large quantities of strong barbiturates along with anticonvulsant drugs such as Phenytoin (Dilantin) and Phenobarbital, which are commonly used to treat seizure disorders and status epileptics.

Taken in small doses, these drugs have few harmful side effects. However, John Jr. was pumped full of these pills. If he wasn't well when he began taking these drugs, he was certainly worse off under their influence. Dilantin, for example, produces a plethora of side effects including gingival hyperplasia of the gums—an uncontrollable growth of rapidly reddening gums that spreads throughout the mouth—and this was not all. This condition was followed by a veritable harvest of problems which reaped in ataxia, nystagmus (involuntary movement of the eyeballs), slurred speech, decreased coordination with an inability to execute fine motor skills or manipulate objects, and unpredictable muscle movements. Not surprisingly, John suffered insomnia, dizziness, transient nervousness and was plagued with headaches, nausea, vomiting, constipation and, quite understandably, chronic depression. To top it all off, he also ran a very high risk of suffering toxic hepatitis and liver damage.

John's father had his own ideas about what caused the seizures, putting it down to malingering in an effort to skip school and gain attention. Marion Gacy thought differently. She knew her boy was ill and she did the best she could to protect him. As an experienced pharmacist, she would have known that her pre-adolescent son was growing steadily more dependent on the painless highs of these mood-altering drugs, and she would have noted the adverse side effects.

However, her main concern was directed at the cease-less friction between the boy and his father. She acted as a buffer to such an extent that John Stanley taunted his son as being a "mamma's boy" and told him he was going to be a "queer." Calling the child a "he-she" was another of his favorite labels of derision.

John was subjected to a pitiless campaign of mental and physical abuse from his bullying father in the years to come. It seemed that a day never passed without the boy getting into trouble. The older Gacy never missed an opportunity to let his son know he was a disappointment, and was always berating the child for the slightest mis-take, calling him "dumb and stupid." This label fixed itself in Johnny's psyche like an unwelcome mantra.

John Jr. loved animals, and at age six, he was given a mutt named Pal. In a drunken rage one day, John Stanley Gacy shot and killed the dog to punish his son, leaving the dead animal on a riverbank where young John found it. The boy stole some flowers from a funeral parlor and gave Pal a proper burial.

The Gacy children enjoyed a Catholic education in the north of the city. Regarded by his teachers as a good stu-dent, John wasn't much liked by his schoolmates. He was overweight, clumsy and inclined to be dreamy and unimaginative. He was ungainly at sports and he wasn't good with his hands, either. Added to this was the fact that he was a sickly child. His mother had told him that he had a heart problem from birth, an "enlarged bottle-neck heart," which kept him away from the rough-and-tumble play of childhood. However, for years doctors could find no evidence of a bad heart. It was not until John was ten that the doctors eventually diagnosed his malady as a form of motor epilepsy. By then, the damage had been done; he had been taking the harmful anti-seizure drugs for five years.

When he was nine, John Wayne claims he fell prey to sexual molestation from a friend of the family who began giving the boy rides in his truck. These trips always included episodes of tickling and wrestling. Invariably, these sessions would end up with the boy's face caught between the man's legs, John claimed. He knew in some way that he was being victimized, but he felt powerless to do anything about it. Telling his father was out of the question.

Around 1952, the Gacy family moved to a more spacious house at 4505 Mamora Street, in the northwest region of Chicago. John later recalled that his father had a "secret place" in this house, the large basement where he would retire to immerse himself in the music of Richard Wagner and drink. The basement was off-limits to the rest of the family, but John Jr. listened in on his father sometimes. Worryingly, when drunk, John Sr. would talk to himself in two different voices.

Before long, young John had found a secret place of his own underneath the front porch where he could see others but not be seen himself. Like his father, who enjoyed his own private den, the boy now had his own secret lair. What he did there was his secret, too. His hiding place was revealed after he stole an item of his mother's underwear and hid it in a paper bag. When the bag was found,

John Jr. was subjected to yet another beating. He then found himself at the wrong end of his father's belt when his younger sister, Karen, found her panties in his bed. After being thrashed by his father, John's mother compounded the punishment by forcing him to wear women's panties to school under his clothes. Later in life, Gacy would explain to interviewers that he had not used the underwear for sexual purposes, as he had previously told his parents. He just liked the feel and smell of it, he said.

Without doubt, John Wayne Michael Gacy staggered with faltering steps into his teens. Abused by his father, he could only rely on the often-misguided support of his mother to protect him. The physical and psychological batterings that John Sr. subjected his son to only ceased when John Sr. died.

At age eleven, young John seemed reasonably settled at school. He had few friends among his peers, but his teachers considered him a good pupil. He was a withdrawn boy who kept to himself, but was not overtly troubled. John's main concern at the time was in trying to live up to his father's high expectations of him, to be a son who shared his father's interests and did things the way he did. To some extent, John did meet some of the criteria—he was always neat and well-dressed, and he kept his room orderly and clean—but his father demanded so much more.

Things came to a head when John Stanley Gacy took his eleven-year-old son on a week's fishing trip to Wisconsin. This was the boy's first real chance to prove himself. Unfortunately, it rained the entire time. The fishing was ruined with the result that Gacy Sr. retired to their tent and drank to excess, all the while brooding and blaming his son for the failed adventure. He never took his son fishing again.

In the same year, John was playing by a swing when he was hit in the head by one of the seats. The accident caused a blood clot in his brain but the trauma wasn't discovered until he was sixteen, when the blackouts ceased after he was prescribed medication to dissolve the blockage.

The tough, brutal, hard-working, hard-drinking perfectionist and disciplinarian that Mr. Gacy was, he admired his own attributes in others, so young John set out to prove he could work hard. It is fair to say that, throughout his life, John Wayne Gacy was a hardworker who never let up. At school, he ran errands for the teachers; he helped the school truant officer by telephoning parents to check up on absentees; at fourteen, he took on odd jobs after school; he had a paper route, and he worked as a stock clerk and delivered groceries for a local store, earning his first salary. He helped his mother paint the house and do chores, and he made sure his homework was always excellent. But this was still not enough in his father's eyes. Nothing the boy did was right.

At the age of seventeen, Gacy was diagnosed with a non-specific heart ailment. He was hospitalized for this problem on several occasions throughout his life. Even so, doctors were never able to find an exact cause for the pain he was suffering. Although John complained frequently about his heart, even more so after his arrest for serial murder, he never suffered any serious heart attack and many thought his "so-called" heart complaint was an attempt to gain sympathy.

Despite his newly diagnosed health problems, 1960 started well for eighteen-year-old John Wayne Gacy. By this age, he had learned that his volunteer work had earned him admiration. Although his father still despised him, John Jr. had at least earned the admiration of his teachers and employers with the help and work he did for them.

Taking his public service impulses further, John formed a civil defense squad at his high school. As the organizer, he awarded himself the rank of captain. He even attached a flashing blue light to the dashboard of his car, and wearing his police-style uniform, he delighted in racing off to fire or traffic incidents. It made him feel important, needed and respected. It gave him a sense of belonging, the kind of acceptance that came with his new responsibilities. It was something he'd sought so frequently from his father at home, to no avail.

In his late teens, it seemed that a friendly and earnest John Wayne Gacy was starting to succeed and move up the social ladder. However, in at least one area, he considered himself an abject failure: He was unable to interact with women.

John was not a naturally attractive youth. With his doughy shape and potato head, he simply didn't appeal to girls. On the rare occasions when he did find himself approaching anything like a sexual encounter, his nerves got the better of him and he failed. On one occasion in his car, he passed out from stress as he was about to get intimate with a girl. The girl had partially stripped and they were groping each other when he fainted. The girl was shocked and Gacy was mortified. When he told his father what had happened, Gacy Sr. was furious with his "weak" son. Once again, he told his son that he was a sissy and a queer. John was distraught, but refused to give up trying to please his father. He gave up on girls and turned his attention instead to politics.

Predictably, this also failed to bring father and son closer together. John began by working as a volunteer for a political candidate in the 45th District of Chicago. For such a young man, he had taken on a great responsibility. Yet despite his success, his father ridiculed him. "Politics is all bullshit," his father ranted, "Politicians are phonies; you are a pansy for working for free." Nevertheless, John loved the work and the long hours. He had found new friends who trusted and admired him. He had also found another home in politics, a place where he was wanted and respected. Here, he could succeed and make his mark, so he dropped out of high school in 1961 at age nineteen. The rift between John and his father widened more than ever before.

John Jr. was aware that his volunteer work was in part motivated by his strained relationship with his father. While on Death Row he commented, "My dad always said I was so stupid, I wouldn't amount to anything, so anything that I got involved with, I always put 100 percent into it, 'cause I figured if you are gonna get involved in something, then do it right. So I was involved in politics, I was involved in community service, and even as young as twenty-two or twenty-three years old, I was honored as Man of the Year in Springfield, Illinois, and was involved in a lot of projects there."

Just like Dean Corll, we could never accuse John Wayne Gacy of being work shy. Despite all his faults, here we find a young man who was driven to hard toil by his brutal and domineering father—not because Mr. Gacy demanded it of his son, but because John wanted to please in any way he could.

Not just content with his political work, John labored away on behalf of the Catholic Church, turning his hand to anything asked of him with zeal. Carrying out repairs, picking up the elderly and dropping them home after services, collecting and delivering their groceries—nothing was too much trouble. In fact, he spent so much time at church that he considered joining the priesthood. He even became a member of the St. John Berchmann's parish bowling team.

John soon recognized that the church was not meeting many of the needs of some parishioners, particularly the young ones. In response, John formed a young adults' group called the Chi Ro Club. He put together social events, ran yard sales to raise cash and scheduled a formal winter dance for his new group. Bearing in mind his later career as a murderer of young men, it is easy to draw the obvious conclusion as to why Gacy formed this club. However, there is no evidence to suggest that anything adverse happened during this time.

Then Gacy's world began to fall apart. During one of his more generous days, it is claimed that Gacy Sr. purchased a new 1960 Chevrolet Impala for his son. It was to become John's pride and joy and he kept it spotless. However, there was a catch. The truth was that Mr. Gacy loaned John the money for the car, and John consequently found himself in debt to his father. John's father now had more control over him than ever before.

After one argument, Gacy Sr. removed the car's distributor cap, saying he would replace it when the payments John owed him were up to date. John was not only humiliated but also inwardly fuming. Unable to get to and from work, carry out his tasks for the church or fulfill his other social obligations, he brooded. After three days, he paid his father back and the distributor part was replaced. But this time, John had had enough. Telling his mother that he was going out to put air in his tires, John left the house and vanished for three months.

Gacy had not even graduated from high school at this point. In fact, he had dropped out of four schools without completing his education at all. He drove to Las Vegas, where he found work as an ambulance driver for the Palm Mortuary and Memorial Park. His employment there was soon terminated when staff discovered that John was too young to drive ambulances; John was just twenty and the minimum legal age was twenty-one. However, rather than lose the enterprising young man, John's boss assigned him to the mortuary. His new job necessitated contact with dead bodies.

Not knowing where her son was, Mrs. Gacy was beside herself with worry. She couldn't sleep. Knowing that John was physically and emotionally sick, she feared for his safety. For his part, John Gacy Sr. could not have cared less, that is until a letter about medical bills from his insurance company dropped through the letterbox.

John had been receiving medical treatment in Las Vegas for his ongoing health problems, and his father was expected to pay the bills. After a few phone calls, it was established that John was living and working in Las

Vegas. The Gacys now knew where their missing son was, but for John Sr. it was all far too late. He was finished with his son.

There was something about the detached, professional way the morticians went about their work that appealed to John Gacy. He found himself fascinated with cadavers and death. The stillness of the corpses, white, bereft of life, skin stretched tight over fragile bone, touched something primitive in him. He learned how the bodies were cleaned, treated and embalmed. Because he had no real lodgings, John slept on the premises at night, which gave him sole access to the dead bodies after everyone else had gone home.

In later years, after his crimes were uncovered, tales began to circulate about what Gacy did in the mortuary with the corpses. Interviewed on Death Row, he indignantly rebutted the rumors: "They got me a job with Palm Mortuary, being the night man picking up dead bodies from all the hospitals and stuff for them. I worked as the night man only. I didn't have nothing to do with the bodies. All this talk that I slept with the dead ones, or had sex with dead bodies, there is no truth to any of that. I lived in the mortuary but not in the embalming room. I mean, it sounds like I slept in the crypts with them. And I never climbed into a coffin, or anything like that. [Laughing]. That is so damned ridiculous. And besides, the dead don't bother you. It is the living you have to worry about."

Alone in a strange city without friends or a social life, John Gacy became a ghoul. When all was secured in the funeral home and the staff had left, he would shuffle over to the cabinets and pull out a drawer. In the weak, yellowy light, he would converse in hushed tones with the corpses, explain his troubles and touch the bodies ever so gently, curiously examining them. Sometimes he would undress them, neatly fold the clothes and leave them next to the caskets. He did this night after night until the director became suspicious and telephoned the Las Vegas police. Although Gacy was never caught in the act, he decided that the time had come to move on and he left his job. After he became a murderer, investigators established that John Gacy was a necrophiliac. He enjoyed having sexual relations with his victims both before and after he killed them, sometimes keeping their bodies around and sleeping with them for a day or so after their deaths. But there is no evidence that Gacy's activities as a necrophiliac began during his time at the mortuary.

Having quit his job at the mortuary, John called his mother and asked her if he could come home. She agreed and John prepared for his homecoming—although it would take him another three months before he could save enough money to make the trip.

By 1963, John Wayne Gacy was back in Chicago. Unable to patch up his relationship with his father, Gacy instead moved in with a maternal uncle and aunt. He was flushed with the newfound confidence he had found by living and working in Las Vegas, and so enrolled in a year-long course at a local business college. Once he completed his studies, Gacy found a position as a management trainee for Nunn Bush, a large shoe company based in Illinois. He turned out to be a born salesman, a hit with the staff and customers alike. Easy going and hardworking, he was soon promoted to departmental manager for the company at the Robinson department store, 821 East Cook Street, near Springfield. At the same time, John discovered the Jaycees—the Junior Chamber of Commerce.

Established in 1920 to provide opportunities for young men to develop personal and leadership skills through services to others, the Jaycees helped set up the U.S. Air Mail service, and have raised millions of dollars for causes such as the Muscular Dystrophy Association of America and the March of Dimes, a charitable organization which fights the growing crisis of premature childbirth in America.

Twenty-one-year-old John Wayne Gacy enrolled in the Jaycees in 1963. John took to the Jaycees like a duck to water. Out of reach of his domineering father, he blossomed. He was now in the company of like-minded young people whose watchwords were "honor" and "achievement." As he had done previously while working as a volunteer for the Catholic Church, John threw himself into the organization with such determination that he won the "Key Man" award for April 1964. This was no small achievement in that he had only been in Springfield for a few months.

Indeed, John was on a roll. He met a young woman, Marlynn Myers, who worked at the Robinson store and they began dating. "It was kinda like love at first sight," he later claimed.

But he then discovered that he had other highly charged feelings. John had been out drinking with a male colleague, a man several years older than himself. At the end of the evening they returned to the man's house for coffee. A homosexual encounter followed in which Gacy received oral sex. After his arrest for murder Gacy admitted somewhat disingenuously, "Although I enjoyed it at first, I felt ashamed and violated. He outsmarted me and I felt used."

Notwithstanding this homosexual encounter, twenty-two-year-old John Wayne Gacy married Marlynn Myers in September 1964. His new father-in-law, Fred Myers, was a successful franchiser of Kentucky Fried Chicken, with outlets in Waterloo, Iowa. John and his wife moved out to Waterloo, where life soon got even better. In 1966, he was named as first Vice President of the Jaycees, the outstanding first-year Jaycee in his area, and the organization's third outstanding member state-wide. His wife also became pregnant with their first child, Christie. To cap things off, his father-in-law put John in charge of three KFC franchises in Waterloo. It seems that Fred Myers was not overly impressed with John as a husband for his Marlynn—he wasn't good breeding stock, Mr. Myers believed—but he doted on his daughter and wanted her to be happy.

John's new job paid $15,000 a year, plus a percentage of the profits. John went on to take a course at the Kentucky Fried Chicken University, joined the Waterloo Jaycees and revelled in the best years of his life.

Following the birth of Gacy's daughter Christie, a son, Michael, followed in 1966. As well as his domestic bliss, Gacy was also working ten- to fourteen-hour days and maintained his devotion to the Jaycees. He organized events, recruited new members, coordinated fundraising efforts and devoted his skills to community projects. At meetings and events, he always arrived with buckets of chicken to hand out in a well-meant public relations exercise. He also had more unorthodox methods of boosting the Jaycees' profile. He recalled, "I moved to Waterloo, Iowa. I was honored as Man of the Year. Besides, apart from working full time, I was Chaplain for the Jaycees, and also ran the membership campaign. Of course, we used pornography and we had stag shows and that's how we increased the membership from 150 to 400 members in that Jaycee Chapter."

Reviving his love of dressing up like a member of the emergency services, John also joined the Waterloo Merchant Patrol, a kind of auxiliary police force set up to protect local businesses. He carried a weapon and even had a red flashing light put on the dashboard of his car.

As time went by, John Gacy's successes mounted. He was voted the Jaycees' outstanding member for 1967, and he was made chaplain of the local organization. In 1968, he just missed out on the Presidency of the Waterloo club. John was the very model of a respectable middle-class businessman. He was married with two adorable children, well-connected politically and commercially, and had a nice house and a secure income. What could possibly go wrong now?

Plenty, it seemed. Even as he went from strength to strength, rumors were spreading around town about Gacy's sexual preferences. It was noted how Gacy always seemed to surround himself with young boys. Everyone in the Jaycees had heard the stories that Gacy was a secret homosexual and that he made passes at the young boys who worked for him at the fast food franchises. Of course, his family and friends refused to believe such things. At least, they did until the spring of 1968, when Gacy's carefully constructed image as a pillar of his local community fell apart in spectacular fashion. In May that year, Gacy was indicted by a grand jury in Black Hawk County for allegedly committing the act of sodomy with a teenage boy named Donald Voorhees.

The story emerged that Gacy was driving alone one night when he heard a young boy call out, "Hey, Mr. Gacy." He pulled his car over and when he realized that it was the son of another Jaycee colleague, he offered him a ride. Don had been at his girlfriend's home and was walking home. Gacy seized the moment to bring up the subject of sex. He mentioned some stag films that several of the Jaycees had allegedly been watching. Don said that he had never seen such a film, and by now Gacy's heart was racing. With Marlynn out of town, he had the house to himself so he invited Don back to his place.

After a few drinks, Gacy manipulated Don into exchanging acts of oral sex. After that night they met several more times for sex. Gacy claimed that these liaisons were at Donald's request and that he paid him some money in return. In March 1968, their "affair" still secret, Donald learned that Gacy was planning to run for Jaycee president and that Donald's own father had been approached by Gacy to act as his campaign manager. This was all too much for Don. Confused and worried about the way Gacy was playing an ever-increasing role in his family, the boy told his father about their relationship. In no time at all, the police were hammering on Gacy's front door.

While executing their search warrant, officers found pornographic videos portraying oral sex. Gacy was charged with sodomy. Voorhees told the courts that Gacy had tricked him into being tied up while visiting Gacy's home a year earlier, and that Gacy had violently raped him. Gacy denied all the charges, claiming that Voorhees had willingly had sexual relations with him in order to earn extra money. Gacy further insisted that Jaycee members opposed to him becoming president of the local chapter were setting him up.

The case was sent to a Grand Jury, where Gacy learned that he was in even more trouble. In late August 1967, another boy named Edward Lynch, a sixteen-year-old employee of one of Gacy's chicken franchises, had been invited to his boss's home while Marlynn was away. Gacy and Lynch went to the basement, where they had a few drinks and played pool. Gacy suggested a bet—that the winner of each frame would give the other oral sex. Lynch agreed and Gacy made sure that he lost the next frame. But Lynch balked when Gacy tried to claim his prize, so instead they retired to the front room and watched some videos. By this time Gacy had become extremely aroused. He produced a knife and ordered Lynch into the master bedroom. The terrified boy tried to run and a scuffle ensued during which Lynch received a few cuts. Gacy appeared to calm down, apologized, and insisted that Lynch watch another video with him. Lynch reluctantly agreed—after all, he was still scared of Gacy, plus he did not want to lose his job.

But as soon as things had calmed, down Gacy took out a padlock and a length of chain. He told Lynch that he wanted to tie him up. Once again, the youth was forced to agree. Gacy secured Lynch and then tried to sit on his lap. Lynch resisted and found himself being strangled by Gacy.

He passed out for a few seconds, and as with the incident with the knife cuts earlier, this seemed to bring Gacy to his senses. He switched back from Mr. Hyde to Dr. Jekyll. He apologized again, untied Lynch and drove him home, insisting that there would be no hard feelings. Despite this, Lynch was fired from his job a few days later.

When this all came out at his Grand Jury hearing, Gacy insisted that Lynch had agreed to a sexual liaison and that much of the sex play had been instigated by the boy in the first place. Determined to brazen things out, Gacy tried to ignore the rumors and the charges against him and persisted in his bid to become president of the Jaycees. He even volunteered to take a lie detector test to prove his innocence to his family and friends. Submitting himself to two polygraphs examinations, he failed both.

Amazingly, many of Gacy's fellow Jaycees *did* rally round him. They refused to believe that such a "fine, upstanding brother" could be a sexual deviant. He stayed in the running for president until he was officially nominated and then, at last, did the decent thing and withdrew from the race, "in the interests of the organization and my family," as he put it in an emotional resignation speech.

Moral support for John Gacy had all but evaporated by now. His wife could hardly hold her head up in public. John's father was incandescent with rage, and Fred Myers was on the verge of sacking his son-in-law. For his part, Gacy thought he could muscle his way out of his problems by the simple expedient of threatening Voorhees's life if he testified against him.

In September, with the court case looming, Gacy hired an eighteen-year-old thug called Russell Schroeder to persuade Voorhees not to testify. Without the star witness, Gacy reasoned that he could beat the rap against him for assaulting Lynch. The police had the chain and padlock, and they had also recovered the stag movies, but John Gacy maintained that there had been no sex, only a fight which had merely been a high-spirited tiff between young men after a drink. With powerful friends and his high standing in the community, Gacy thought he would win hands down. He convinced himself that he would be able to resume his social life and business life as if nothing had ever happened.

For his part, Schroeder jumped at the chance to earn the $300 offered by Gacy for his services. It was money he could well use to pay off the loan on his car. He approached Voorhees, who refused to take him seriously. Undeterred, Schroeder sprayed Voorhees with Mace, burning his face. Vorhees ran home in agony. His parents took him to the hospital and reported the incident to the police. Schroeder was brought in for questioning and quickly implicated Gacy. Instead of going away, Gacy's troubles had suddenly got a whole lot worse.

As the investigation into the sodomy charge was being prepared, other witnesses lost their fear of Gacy and came forward. At the front of the line was seventeen-year-old Richard Westphal. He had worked for Gacy and he told investigators that Gacy had often played pool with him, the prize being oral sex, which the youth declined. Gacy had also coerced his wife, Marlynn, into sleeping with Westphal, who was a virgin. After they had finished in bed, Gacy walked into the room saying that the boy "owed him one."

An eighteen-year-old boy who worked at the same restaurant as Westphal also came forward to report that Gacy had threatened him with a pistol, forcing him to play a bluff game of Russian roulette because the boy had talked to Westphal and knew too much about Gacy's perverted sex life. Then, a fifteen-year-old youth emerged to claim that Gacy paid him and other boys $5 each to help out in "sex experiments," which he claimed he was conducting for the Governor of Iowa.

At just twenty-six years old, John Wayne Gacy was ruined.

As with the majority of sex offenders, the courts may order that a defendant attend a psychiatric hospital for evaluation prior to a court case. Gacy could not make the $10,000 bail bond so he was sent to the Psychopathic Hospital at the State University of Iowa to await his trial. There, he was examined over a period of seventeen days. Apart from being overweight, the doctors could not find anything physically wrong with him.

Dr. LD Amick was one of the psychiatrists assigned to Gacy at that time. He found that Gacy had an IQ of 118, which was "bright and normal." But the doctor also concluded that Gacy suffered from a total denial of responsibility for anything that went wrong in his life. He had an excuse for every accusation; he would twist the truth about every wayward move to deflect blame from himself. However convicting the circumstances, Gacy would always try to find a way to make himself look good.

In regard to the accusations of molesting boys, Dr. Amick wrote in his trial report that Gacy had "no remorse over his admitted deeds." He went on, "We regard Mr.

Gacy as an antisocial personality, a diagnostic term for individuals who are basically unsocialized and whose behavior pattern brings them repeatedly into conflict with society." Dr. Amick concluded, "No known medical treatment can help such people because they do not learn from experience."

In failing to raise his son adequately, in neglecting to "socialize" him with his peers, it can be argued that John Stanley Gacy, Sr. had much to answer for. His treatment of his son had contributed to the creation of a sexual psychopath, a young man who would later turn into a creature of monstrous proportions.

Days before his trial, Gacy changed his mind and decided to throw himself at the mercy of the court. He pled guilty to the sodomy charge. This was a calculated move by Gacy to try to escape a prison sentence, and he almost succeeded. Investigating probation officer Jack Harker had been so impressed by Gacy's convincing manner that he supported John, arguing that a period of supervised probation would serve just as well as any prison term. Also in Gacy's favor was the fact this was his first offense and that he had agreed to move back to Illinois, far away from Iowa.

Judge Peter Van Merte had been a sitting judge for years. He was a no-nonsense hardliner who had heard this sort of thing many times before. Sitting patiently while the defense made its argument in favor of a lighter sentence, the judge thought long and hard about John's abuse of his position at work, and how the respected Jaycees had been brought into disrepute in his own city. The judge took a very dim view of the accused, more so because there seemed to be a pattern of molestation that, if not stopped now, would only escalate.

To exacerbate the issue, Gacy was not an Iowa native. He was an out-of-town city slicker, a man who used his position in the judge's own community to abuse young boys.

The judge sentenced Gacy to ten years in the grimly ornate Iowa State Reformatory for Men at Anamosa, twenty-five miles east of Cedar Rapids. That very same day, Marlynn Gacy filed for divorce. She later remarried, and John Wayne Gacy would never see his wife and children again.

Prisoner 26526, John Wayne Gacy, threw himself into prison life with the same degree of enthusiasm as he had his volunteer work on the outside. Not a day passed without Gacy organizing and doing something. He passed the examinations for a high school diploma, something he had failed to achieve as a youth, and took college credits in psychology. Setting out to impress inmates and staff alike, John toiled in the prison kitchen and was thrilled to find that the facility had a Jaycee chapter. Working all the hours allocated to him, he spearheaded the design and building of a miniature golf course for the inmates' use, and prepared Jaycee banquets. He won a number of Jaycee honors, including the club's "Sound Citizens Award," and he took on the roles of chaplain and legal counsel. Gacy proved that he could be well-behaved and responsible—in a controlled environment, at least.

While he was in jail, Gacy lost his father. John Stanley Gacy died of cirrhosis of the liver on Christmas Day, 1969. The man had been completely broken by his son's crimes and the disgrace John had heaped on his family. Several times, John Sr. had been reduced to tears—the only times he had cried in his life.

Somewhat shamefully, Gacy served just eighteen months of his ten-year sentence. He was released on Thursday, June 18, 1970, and his parole was finally discharged on Tuesday, October 19, 1971. On his release from Anamosa, the prison warden shook Gacy's hand, explaining that he had been a model prisoner and that he was sad to see him go.

A free man, Gacy traveled to Chicago, moving back in with his mother, who now lived in a new condominium. Finding work as a cook at a popular restaurant called Bruno's, his employment brought him into contact with members of the Chicago Black Hawks hockey team and a number of Cook County police officers, many of whom he befriended.

In February 1971, and having only been out of prison for eight months, twenty-nine-year-old Gacy was in trouble once again. He picked up a teenager near the Greyhound bus station and tried to force him to have sex. Gacy would later claim, once again, that it was the boy's fault. The youth, he alleged, had offered sex. Gacy was arrested and charged with assault, but the case was dismissed when the complainant failed to show up in court. Gacy had escaped another prison sentence by the skin of his teeth. Had he been found guilty, thirty-three young men may not have lost their lives.

By the time his parole period had expired, Gacy had befriended a young street hustler named Mickel Reid. They had met on a street corner as early as November 1970 while Gacy was trawling for sex. The two men set up a home maintenance business called PDM Contractors (Property Development Maintenance Contractors), a name that John's mother had suggested. To everyone's surprise, business boomed, and Gacy and his mother bought a three-bedroom, ranch-style house at 8213 West Summerdale Avenue, Des Plaines, to accommodate the growing company. John owned one-half of the property, while his mother and two sisters owned the other 50 percent.

Once the house had been purchased, Gacy allowed Mickel Reid to move in, as well as one of Gacy's former co-workers at Bruno's, a boy called Roger. Like most of Gacy's homosexual liaisons, his relationship with Reid was destined to fail. Gacy, at heart, was unable to accept his own homosexuality and this led to him manifesting unusual and unprovoked violent behavior. One evening, when Gacy and Reid were working in the garage that adjoined the property, Gacy struck Reid over the head with a hammer. Shocked and bloodied, Reid managed to collect himself as Gacy raised his hammer to strike another blow. Reid fought him off and Gacy calmed down. Gacy apologized but the terrified youth left the house immediately, taking Roger with him.

If we are to believe Gacy, his first murder was committed on New Year's Day in 1972. John, now thirty, had joined his mother at a family party. John was drinking heavily at the party and sat around brooding as the night wore on. Eventually, he climbed into his car and drove off into the night. "I just went looking around," he told the police later. Gacy ended up at Chicago's Greyhound bus station, where he spotted a fair-haired youth whom he remembered as "The Greyhound Bus Boy." Tim McCoy was from Omaha, Nebraska, and had just arrived in Illinois. Gacy invited him back to his house where they had drinks and sandwiches, followed by sex. According to Gacy's later statement—which can be safely taken with a pinch of salt—he retired to his own room and Tim slept in the guest room.

Gacy said that he awoke to find the youth walking toward him brandishing a butcher knife. He claimed that in the ensuing struggle the boy fell on the knife and stabbed himself to death. In a second version of the story, Gacy claimed that the boy didn't fight back; rather, Tim seemed surprised and frightened. As Gacy grappled for the knife, he was accidentally cut on the left forearm and felt "a surge of power from my toes to my brain." Then he said he plunged the knife into Tim's chest. "When it was all over," Gacy claimed, "I looked down at the pants he'd worn to bed. They were covered with blood—but with something else too. During the struggle I had experienced a powerful sexual release."

After the stabbing, Gacy was faced with the problem of how to dispose of the body. He did not feel that anyone would believe that he had acted in self-defense, so he cleaned up the blood, dragged the body to the foyer closet, opened the crawlspace trapdoor and pushed it through. He would bury it later. However, the truth of why the boy was walking towards Gacy with a knife soon became clear. When Gacy went into the kitchen he found on the work surface a carton of eggs and a joint of unsliced bacon. The young guest had not been planning murder; he was preparing breakfast for his host.

But the boy was dead—and Gacy had got away with it. Six months later, however, his sexual conduct did land him in trouble. On June 22, 1972, Northbrook Police brought Gacy in on charges of aggravated battery and reckless conduct SOL (stricken on leave to reinstate). The incident stemmed from an accusation that Gacy had fought with one of his sex partners, then attempted to run the boy down with his car.

It transpired that, posing as a police officer, Gacy had lured the young man into his car and handcuffed him. After a short conversation, Gacy said, "What's it worth to you to get out of this?" When the lad explained that he didn't have much money, Gacy asked, "Would you suck my dick?"

Fearing for his life, the passenger consented. Gacy drove to the restaurant where he worked and forced the boy into the bathroom. It was between 3:30 and 4:30 a.m. Once inside the building, the boy resisted Gacy's attempts to make him perform oral sex and he was hit in the head several times and kicked. Somehow, handcuffed though he was, the boy managed to open the door to the bathroom and ran off down the road. Gacy followed in his car and knocked him down.

The victim survived to testify, but the overworked court system offered Gacy a plea bargain and the charge was reduced to the status of "stricken on leave to reinstate." This meant that Gacy had been issued with a warning and that if he were brought in front of the courts again the charge would be reinstated. Once again, the criminal justice system failed the community. Another pre-emptive opportunity to end Gacy's murderous career had been missed.

On July 1, 1972, just nine days after being charged with this latest offense, John Wayne Gacy married a woman named Carole Lofgren. Gacy and Carole had known each other since schooldays. Carole, herself recently divorced, found John "a very warm, understanding person, easy to talk to." She claimed that he was comforting to her and her two daughters, four-year-old Tammy and two-year-old April, from her first marriage. Carole also accepted the fact that Gacy was, as he admitted to her, bisexual.

Of course, there was much more to Gacy's psyche than confused sexuality. He truly was a Jekyll and Hyde character. His mind had split in two. On the one hand, there was Gacy the successful contractor, community builder, event organizer and friendly neighbor; on the other hand, he was a sexual pervert, a sexual sadist whose murderous compulsions were growing out of control. A power struggle was raging inside John Wayne Gacy—and it would be the killer, the Mr. Hyde, that would come out on top to turn him into one of the most heinous serial murderers of all time.

Following their marriage, Carole, her two daughters and her mother, Jean Cienciwa, moved into Gacy's home on West Summerdale. Carole would later tell police that she was aware that he had been married previously and had two children—and that he had been in trouble in Iowa. She had believed John when he told her that the charges were primarily for pornography. She knew nothing of the sodomy charges. Had she known the truth, no doubt she would have never have married him.

Initially, Carole's two girls were pleased to be around John Gacy. They tried hard to please him and were readily affectionate, climbing into his lap to tell him of their day's activities. However, Carole soon saw that Gacy failed to reciprocate her childrens' affection. In time, Tammy and April stopped trying to win over their new father. Gacy was, of course, mirroring the lack of affection shown to him by his own father, but Carole was not to know this. Even if she had, it would not have made her new husband's rejection of her children any easier to bear. At this early stage in their marriage, all was not well between John Gacy and Carole.

After John Gacy's arrest for murder, Detective Lieutenant Joseph Kozenczak and Detective Greg Bedoe spoke to Carole at length. She recalled that her husband's unusual behavior didn't stop with his lack of interest in her daughters, and that it was not uncommon for John to lounge around the bedroom, naked, and to masturbate while flicking through homosexual magazines. When she taunted him, he would push her across the room. There were pornographic magazines everywhere, even under the kitchen sink. She found semen-stained silk bikini male underwear behind the bedroom dresser and under their bed. Initially, she thought that he was trying to arouse her, but she rapidly noticed other unusual activities involving her husband. He would stay out late and would occasionally pull his car into the driveway with its lights out, silently climbing out and heading straight into the garage. He often had a young blond-haired boy with him.

Carole was scared. Although she loved John, she could not help being suspicious of him. She told the detectives that on one occasion she took the key to the garage and looked inside. What she found shocked her. The interior had been gaudily decorated. There were mattresses over the floor, red lights plugged into the walls and mirrors on the ceiling. There was something else, too. The new bride could smell a strange, sickly-sweet odor emanating from the crawlspace beneath the house. She confided in a friendly neighbor, a Mrs. Grexas, who told her a rat had probably died under the floor. John blamed the stench on the dampness.

On one occasion, Carole claimed she awoke around 4:00 a.m. after hearing John's car entering the driveway. When John turned on the light, Carole's presence in the living room startled him. He became angry and ordered her back to bed. She asked him what he was doing but he became madder, so she retired without pushing things any further. After all, it was not uncommon for John to arrive home in the early hours of the morning and sleep on the couch in the recreation room, which he had fitted out with a bar and a pool table.

Carole later learned that John was having sex with some of the young men who worked at his construction company. However, not all of these men were compliant sexual partners. In fact, one able-bodied young man actually beat up John in his driveway after Gacy attempted to rape him. Gacy told Carole the assault had been a dispute over money.

Despite his bizarre and depraved domestic behavior, by 1974 Gacy had well and truly ingratiated himself into the community. He was generally popular and was always willing to help his neighbors out. His social standing improved even more when he began to host his theme parties. One memorable event had a Hawaiian luau theme, while another had a cowboy flavor. Around 300 guests were usually invited to the parties, which were held on Independence Day, July 4. A John Wayne Gacy party was usually the talk of the town.

Slowly but surely, Gacy was making his way back up the social ladder. At one function—the groundbreaking of a new retirement center for the elderly that Gacy had helped raise money for—John had his photograph taken with the then mayor, Michael Bilandic. Gacy could never aspire to such a high office because of his criminal record, but he was able to nourish his longstanding taste for politics by nonetheless associating with powerful figures such as Bilandic.

Given his social-climbing aspirations, it was not long before Gacy caught the attention of Robert F. Matwick, the Democratic township committee member for Norwood Park. Gacy and Matwick met when Gacy and his employees volunteered to clean up Matwick's Democratic Party headquarters. Before long, in 1975, Gacy was appointed to his first political post, that of Secretary Treasurer of the Norwood Park Township Street Lighting District. Another honor followed when he was chosen to march at the head of Chicago's Polish Constitution Day Parade. He also ran the River Grove Moose Lodge (now thirty-three, he was too old to be a Jaycee). As part of the Moose Lodge's Jolly Jokers Club, Gacy further impressed Matwick by dressing up as a clown to entertain children at parties and hospitals. This was something Gacy especially liked to do. He invented two clown characters, Pogo and Patches, and later explained that, "Pogo was the happy clown while Patches was more serious." Even when creating happy fantasy characters, there was still an element of Jekyll and Hyde to Gacy's way of thinking.

Yet even as Gacy attempted to re-climb the social and political ladder, trouble dogged him once more. The old rumors about his homosexual interest in young boys resurfaced even as Gacy ingratiated himself with Matwick and his political friends. While he was cleaning the Democratic Party headquarters, Gacy was accused by sixteen-year-old fellow volunteer Tony Antonucci of making unwanted sexual advances towards him. He only backed off, the accusation ran, when Antonucci threatened to hit Gacy with a chair.

One month later, Gacy invited Antonucci to his home, where he tricked the young man into putting on a pair of handcuffs. Once Antonucci was safely locked up, Gacy began to undress him. Fortunately, Antonucci was able to free himself and wrestle Gacy to the ground, where he in turn managed to handcuff his attacker. He agreed to let the older man go once he had extracted from Gacy a promise to never touch him again. Gacy honored his promise, and the boy remained working for Gacy for another a year following the incident.

At his station house in Chicago, Detective Joe Kozenczak revealed to author Christopher Berry-Dee that one of the most significant things Carole had told him was related to an event that took place on Mother's Day in 1975. John had risen early and told her that he was going to give her a Mother's Day gift, and that when he had done so he would tell her something interesting. He initiated intercourse with Carole, and once they had finished he announced that she should never expect to have sex with him again. "I am through with women," he told her. This was John Wayne Gacy's Mother's Day gift to his wife. True to his word, Gacy never made love to Carole again.

After this incident, any remaining inhibitions John had about commenting on young men and their bodies in front of Carole fell away. John and Carole would be in a bar and John would comment on a "guy's tight ass" or he would openly describe the type of young man that turned him on. It was clear to Carole that their marriage had broken down and she asked him for a divorce. Gacy readily agreed. He even sent her to his own lawyer, to speed things along, and helped Carole to move out of the family home. Carole and Gacy's divorce was finalized on March 2, 1976. They met for dinner once or twice after this, but Carole eventually remarried and stopped seeing her former husband altogether.

Following Carole's departure, John Wayne Gacy's murderous impulses spiraled out of control. The majority of his victims were killed over the next two years, until his final arrest in late December 1978. Gacy's life of crime ended when police investigating the disappearance of fifteen-year-old Robert Piest were told that the last time he had been seen was with Gacy outside a drugstore. Investigators looked into Gacy's record, saw his previous charge for sodomy and decided to obtain a warrant to search his home. Their initial search provided no definite evidence of Gacy's crimes, but the police told Gacy that they would return for a more extensive investigation the following day. Realizing that the game was up, on December 22, 1978, John Wayne Gacy confessed to the murders of his many victims.

There can be no doubt that John Wayne Gacy was emotionally stunted as a child. This inhibited his mental development to the extent that he effectively had a divided conscience. From birth through adolescence, his most formative years, John's mind split in two. He developed two differing sets of thinking processes, two sets of values, attitudes, emotions and aspirations that he carried through to adult life. On the one hand, he was a hardworking, honest, upright pillar of the community with social and political aspirations; on the other hand, he harbored dark and perverted secrets. Mr. Hyde was never far from the surface.

Sexually confused, John had many issues in regard to women. He loved his mother, but probably saw her as a strong, gregarious woman who became weak. He watched as his father systematically broke her spirit, heaping physical and mental abuse upon her. Gacy hated what he saw, but at the same time wanted to please his distant father and be like him. Subconsciously, John Wayne Gacy had little respect for women in general, and this can be described as an extension of his father's specific lack of respect for John's mother.

It is interesting to note that, despite his estranged relationship with his father, John was devastated when he died. He was equally distraught that, because he was in prison, John was not allowed to attend his father's funeral. On the very day that he was arrested, John was on his way to visit his father's grave, where he intended to place a rosary—and possibly commit suicide.

John Gacy, Sr. was a control freak and a perfectionist. It is no coincidence that John Jr. would become a perfectionist in his work and a control freak, too. He aimed for perfection in organizing social events, and his dedication to fine detail and long hours gained him high recognition with the Jaycees.

Gacy carried on this perfectionist streak while in prison for the first time. He designed and organized the construction of the inmates' mini-golf course, for example. He also worked on his education, finally finishing high school, and worked his way up to several positions of trust, such as prison chaplain and legal counsel. Locked up, Gacy was a thoughtful, giving individual. It was only in the outside world that his taste for sexual abuse, torture and murder came to the fore.

It can be argued that the treatment John dished out to his victims was an echo of the treatment he had received from his father. The victims, in a sense, were all John himself. In this scenario, he became his own father, exercising power and control over his victims and punishing them for his own weaknesses in mind, body and soul.

It is also of some interest to note that John never assaulted a woman, nor did he ever attack older males—though this can in part be explained by the fact that he was too much of a coward to target mature men. His targets were young male prostitutes and runaways, the innocent and often gullible.

But if John thought so little of women, why did he marry? It is not hard to find the answer: It was the socially acceptable thing to do. The "good" John Gacy desperately wanted to fit in, to be a respectable pillar of society. Marriage and children meant that he was "normal," that he had conquered the "bad" John Gacy who was struggling for control of his soul. He was deluded, of course. The "bad" John Gacy was always with him and both of John's marriages failed when this "bad" side came to the fore.

His first wife quite justifiably left him when he was sent to prison. His second wife left him when he made it clear to her that he was a committed homosexual. It could be argued that the failure of John's second marriage was a conscious act on his part. With his first marriage, John was essentially living a lie. He still had political aspirations at the time. By his second marriage, John's dreams of high office were gone forever. Once he had established his building contractor's business and cemented his standing in the community, Carole and her children were effectively surplus to requirements. He drove Carole away so that the real John Gacy could come to the foreground. Unfortunately, the "real" John Gacy was a twisted, murdering monster.

John would later claim that an alter ego, which he called "Mad Jack," committed the murders. Looking back, it does appear that Gacy had an alter ego of sorts, though this was never medically proven. Mad Jack was based on a police officer named Jack Hanley whom Gacy had once tried to befriend. Hanley was a detective with the Cook County hit-and-run unit and was all the things Gacy was not: muscular, commanding and a devoted hater of homosexuals. Jack Hanley was the punishing type of lawman that Gacy both admired and feared. He became a kind of obsession figure for Gacy, an alter ego— and later, a scapegoat.

It has been claimed that when John started drinking or taking drugs, Mad Jack would take over and do things that

Gacy would never do when sober. Gacy would eventually confess to police that when he couldn't really remember the details of many of his murders, such as what he had done with some of the bodies before he buried them, it was because Jack had been in charge during the commission of the crimes. However, this explanation does not fit with the John Gacy we have met so far. John Wayne Gacy was soliciting sex with young men and committing serious sexual offenses long before he met Jack Hanley.

Gacy was an individual who used his role as the manager of several fried chicken outlets to procure young boys, and he used the same technique and opportunity when working in politics and around the community. It is more than likely, though, that drugs and drink fueled the sexual cravings that he already held. Like so many serial murderers, Gacy never accepted the blame for his actions—it was always, without exception, the fault of "Mad Jack," or the boys themselves.

There are many observers who argue that John did not have a conscience. We contend that the "good" John Gacy had a conscience, and the work and honors he gained working for the community are testimony to this. Conversely, the "bad" John Gacy had no conscience whatsoever, and tragically, the "bad" John Gacy prevailed during the last few years of his freedom.

JOHN GACY'S VICTIMS

Gacy is thought to have murdered at least thirty-three young men. Not all the details are known for each victim. The information below refers to those we have the most information for, especially in relation to autopsy and coroner reports as indicated by the Body Number and Medical Examiner Number for each victim.

John Butkovich
Body No. 2, Medical Examiner No. 1065
Cloth-like material on throat
Male, white, 5 feet 9 inches, 150 pounds
Last seen: July 29, 1975, Chicago, Illinois
Identified: December 29, 1978

Darrell Sampson
Body No. 29, Medical Examiner No. 494
Cloth-like material on throat
Male, white, 5 feet 5 inches, 140 pounds
Last seen: April 6, 1976, Chicago, Illinois
Identified: November 18, 1979
Age: eighteen

Samuel Stapleton
Body No. 6, Medical Examiner No. 1274
Male, white, 5 feet 6 inches, 145 pounds
Last seen: May 14, 1976, Chicago, Illinois
Identified: November 14, 1979
Age: fourteen

Randall Reffert
Body No. 7, Medical Examiner No. 1277
Cloth-like material on throat
Male, white, 5 feet 9 inches, 145 pounds
Last seen: May 14, 1976, Chicago, Illinois

Identified: Spring 1979
Age: fifteen

Michael Bonnin
Body No. 18, Medical Examiner No. 1379
Ligature around the neck
Male, white, 5 feet 7 inches, 150 pounds
Last seen: June 3, 1976, Chicago, Illinois
Identified: January 6, 1979
Age: seventeen

Billy Carroll, Jr.
Body No. 22, Medical Examiner No. 1439
Cloth-like material on throat
Male, white, 5 feet 8 inches, 160 pounds
Last seen: June 13, 1976, Chicago, Illinois
Identified: March 17, 1979
Age: sixteen

Rick Johnson
Body No. 23, Medical Examiner No. 1452
Male, white, 5 feet 6 inches, 130 pounds
Last seen: August 6, 1976, Chicago, Illinois
Identified: December 29, 1978
Age: seventeen

Gregory Godzik
Male, white, 5 feet 9 inches, 140 pounds
Last seen: December 12, 1976, Chicago, Illinois
Age: seventeen

Gacy recalled that seventeen-year-old Gregory Godzik loved his job with PDM Contractors. His worked involved a range of unskilled tasks, such as cleaning work. The money he earned allowed him to buy parts for his 1966 Pontiac car, a time-consuming hobby. On December 12, 1976, Gregory dropped his date off at her house, a girl he had had a crush on for some while, and told her he was going home.

In fact, he had a prior engagement to deliver some marijuana to Gacy at home. As it turned out, he wasn't able to buy any drugs and went to Gacy's house to let him know. In Gacy's account of what happened next, he retired to bed and when he woke up the next morning he found Gregory dead, sitting in a chair and wearing only his underwear. A rope was tied around his neck. Gacy disposed of the body in the crawlspace beneath his house.

Gregory's parents reported their son as missing on December 13, 1976, and the police recovered his car that same day. His body was not recovered until after Gacy's arrest.

Robert Donnelly (survived)

Towards the end of December 1977, nineteen-year-old department store employee Robert Donnelly was walking along a northwest Chicago street on his way to a bus stop when a black Oldsmobile pulled over to the curb. The boy suddenly found himself fixed in a spotlight shining from the driver's side of the car. It was Gacy, playing the part of a tough cop. He asked the boy for identification and then pointed a gun at his head, shouting, "Get in or I'll blow you away."

Placing handcuffs on the young man, he drove him back to West Summerdale, forced whisky down his throat and then anally raped him. Gacy then dragged Robert into the bathroom and repeatedly dunked his head into a bathtub full of water until the boy lost consciousness.

After Robert came to, Gacy urinated on him, dragged him back into the recreation room to watch homosexual movies and continued the torture. Donnelly later testified in court that Gacy made him play Russian roulette with a revolver, spinning the cylinder and pulling the trigger ten to fifteen times until the gun finally went off. It was loaded with a blank round.

Gacy then bound and gagged his terrified victim and raped him again. His rage nearly spent, Gacy ordered the weakened youth to take a shower and get dressed, then put him in the car for what he promised would be Donnelly's last ride.

"How's it feel, knowing you're going to die?," Gacy taunted as he drove Donnelly back downtown. But then, inexplicably, Gacy released his captive with one last threat. "If you go to the cops I'll hunt you down."

However, Donnelly did go to the police. He described Gacy's black car, with its distinctive personalized "PDM" number plate. Police interviewed Gacy, who told them that the incident had happened, but that it was part of a consensual master-and-servant sex game. The prosecutor who reviewed the case dropped it on the grounds that it was one person's word against another. This would not be the only time that Gacy would be allowed to go free after committing similar attacks. He was arrested and released on three separate occasions following complaints against him by terrified youths.

John Szyc

Body No. 3, Medical Examiner No. 1121
Male, white, 5 feet 9 inches, 130 pounds
Last seen: January 20, 1977, Chicago, Illinois
Identified: January 6, 1979
Age: nineteen

John Prestidge

Body No. 1, Medical Examiner No. 1066
Male, white, 6 feet, 165 pounds
Last seen: March 15, 1977, Chicago, Illinois
Identified: January 6, 1979
Age: twenty

Jeff D. Rignall (survived)

Jeff Rignall, a twenty-six-year-old homosexual, was walking to a Chicago gay bar when Gacy picked him up in his black Oldsmobile. Though Rignall climbed into Gacy's car willingly, Gacy chloroformed him for the drive back to West Summerdale Avenue. There, he stripped the man and strapped him to what the victim would later describe to the police as a pillory device that held his head and arms immobile. His attacker then forced him to perform oral sex and repeatedly raped him with a number of blunt objects. At one point, according to Rignall, there was another person in the room who participated in the sodomy, but he never saw the man's face.

Rignall was later dumped in the snow at the base of the Alexander Hamilton statue in a downtown Chicago park. He was bleeding from the rectum and his face felt as if it was on fire. He spent several days in a hospital and tests would later show that he had suffered facial burns and liver damage from the chloroform.

When Rignall tried to press charges against Gacy, the police rapidly lost interest once they found out that the complainant was homosexual. Rignall then decided to sue Gacy and hired a civil lawyer. Gacy counter-sued, claiming that Rignall had verbally abused and pushed him. Gacy eventually settled the suit for $3,000, once again escaping proper punishment.

Matthew Bowman
Body No. 8, Medical Examiner No. 1278
Ligature around neck
Male, white, 5 feet 8 inches, 140 pounds
Last seen: July 5, 1977, Crystal Lake, Illinois
Identified: January 29, 1979
Age: nineteen

Robert Gilroy
Body No. 25, Medical Examiner No. 1454
Cloth-like material in his throat
Male, white, 6 feet, 175 pounds
Identified: January 6, 1979
Age: eighteen

John Mowery
Body No. 20, Medical Examiner No. 1382
Ligature around his neck
Male, white, 5 feet 8 inches, 145 pounds
Last seen: September 25, 1977, Chicago, Illinois
Identified: January 27, 1979

Russell L. Nelson
Body No. 16, Medical Examiner No. 1377
Cloth-like material in his throat
Male, white, 5 feet 7inches
Last seen: October 17, 1977, Chicago, Illinois
Age: twenty-one

Robert Winch
Body No. 11, Medical Examiner No. 322
Rope around his neck
Male, white, 5 feet 7 inches, 145 pounds
Last seen: November 10, 1977, Kalamazoo, Michigan
Identified: September 11, 1979
Age: sixteen

Tommy Boling
Body No. 12, Medical Examiner No. 1323
Ligature around his neck
Male, white, 5 feet 8 inches, 145 pounds
Last seen: November 18, 1977, Chicago, Illinois
Age: twenty

David Talma
Body No. 17, Medical Examiner No. 1378

Ligature around neck
Male, white, 6 feet
Last seen: December 9, 1977, Chicago, Illinois
Identified: November 16, 1979

William Kindred
Body No. 27, Medical Examiner No. 1456
Cloth-like material on his throat
Male, white, 5 feet 8 inches, 155 pounds
Last seen: January 1978, Chicago, Illinois
Identified: May 16, 1979

Timothy O'Rourke
Male, white, 5 feet 7 inches, 135 pounds
Last seen: Spring 1978, Chicago, Illinois
Indentified: January 9, 1979
Age: twenty-one

Frank Landingan
Cloth-like material in the throat
Male, white, 5 feet 3 inches, 119 pounds
Last seen: November 4, 1978, Chicago, Illinois
Identified: November 14, 1978
Age: twenty

James Mazzara
Male, white, 5 feet 2 inches, 140 pounds
Last seen: Thanksgiving 1978, Elmwood Park, Illinois
Identified: December 20, 1978
Age: twenty

Robert Jerome Piest
Body No. 30, Medical Examiner No. 231
Paper-like material in the throat
Male, white, 5 feet 8 inches, 140 pounds
Last seen: December 11, 1978, Des Plaines, Illinois
Identified: April 9, 1979
Age: fifteen

FBI HIGH RISK REGISTER—JOHN WAYNE GACY

1. Alcohol abuse
2. Drug abuse
3. Psychiatric history
4. Criminal history
5. Sexual problems
6. Physical abuse
7. Psychological abuse
8/9. Dominant father figure aligned with a negative relationship with male caretaker figures
10. Negative relationships with both natural mother and or adoptive mother
11. Treated unfairly
12. Head trauma
13. Demon Seed

1	2	3	4	5	6	7	8/9	10	11	12	13	%
X	X	X	X	X	X	X	XX	0	X	X	?	84.5

Other Books from Ulysses Press

Online Killers: Portraits of Murderers, Cannibals and Sex Predators Who Stalked the Web for Their Victims
Christopher Barry-Dee and Steven Morris, $14.95
The Internet has rapidly become an integral part of everyone's life—including the most violent criminals. *Online Killers* chronicles the stories of the sinister individuals who have used the Web to work unimaginable evil from the privacy of their own homes.

Serial Killers: Up Close and Personal
Inside the World of Torturers, Psychopaths and Mass Murderers
Christopher Berry-Dee, $15.95
The headline-grabbing crime. The grizzly facts in the coroner's report. The shocking revelations from the trial. *Serial Killers: Up Close and Personal* provides all these details plus one more: the murderer's first-person perspective. Revealing quotes from convicted killers add an even more frightening element to these chilling accounts.

Serial Killers and Mass Murderers: Profiles of the World's Most Barbaric Criminals
Nigel Cawthorne, $14.95
Even the world's most depraved murderers were once only known as somebody's neighbor or somone's son. What turned these people into killers? In one chilling chapter after another, this book profiles a terrifying succession of homicidal maniacs. *Serial Killers and Mass Murderers* presents a fascinating investigation of the dark side.

The Six Unsolved Ciphers: Inside the Mysterious Codes That Have
Confounded the World's Greatest Cryptographers
Richard Belfield, $14.95
This book brings to life the amazing stories and fascinating
structures of the secret codes that have stubbornly resisted the efforts
of the world's best code-breakers and most powerful decryption
software. Readers will follow the horrific story of the Zodiac serial
killer and see reproductions of his symbol-filled letters.

Solomon's Builders: Freemasons, Founding Fathers and the Secrets
of Washington, D.C.
Christopher Hodapp, $14.95
Solomon's Builders guides readers on a Freemason's tour of
Washington, D.C. as it separates fact from myth and reveals the background of the sequel to *The Da Vinci Code*. This book transports the
reader back to the birth of a radical new nation and tells how a secret
society influenced and inspired the formation of what would become
the most powerful nation on earth.

Atheist Universe: The Thinking Person's Answer to Christian
Fundamentalism
David Mills, $14.95   *Foreword by Dorion Sagan*
Clear, concise and persuasive, *Atheist Universe* details exactly
why God is unnecessary to explain the universe and life's diversity,
organization and beauty.

To order these books call 800-377-2542 or 510-601-8301, fax 510-
601-8307, e-mail ulysses@ulyssespress.com, or write to Ulysses Press,
P.O. Box 3440, Berkeley, CA 94703. All retail orders are shipped free of
charge. California residents must include sales tax. Allow two to three weeks
for delivery.

Christopher Berry-Dee is the editor-in-chief of *The New Criminologist*. His books include *Talking with Serial Killers* and *Dad, Help Me*, the story of Derek Bentley and Christopher Craig. He has also worked on TV crime programs.

Steve Morris is the editor of *The New Criminologist*, a documentary true crime consultant and TV researcher. An international authority on the study of serial murder and sex crime, he is the author of several books and related publications.